TANDRIDGE GOLF CLUB

THE FIRST 75 YEARS

Tandridge Golf Club

The First 75 Years

A History by the late Tony Englefield
Updated by John Wilson

VERTUE PUBLISHING

© Tandridge Golf Club 1999

First Edition
July 1999

Typeset and published by
Vertue Publishing
Kent Hatch Road
Limpsfield Chart
Oxted   Surrey   RH8 0SZ

Tel   01883 730270
Fax   01883 730570

Printed by
Antony Rowe Ltd.
Bumper's Farm
Chippenham
Wilts. SN14 6LH

Tel   01249 659705
Fax   01249 443103

ISBN 1 902125 02 9

Contents

PREFACE 1

FOREWORDS 3

CHAPTER 1
Origin and Formation 5

CHAPTER 2
The Fire 17

CHAPTER 3
Bert Morris 21

CHAPTER 4
The Course 25

CHAPTER 5
The Clubhouse and Other Buildings 35

CHAPTER 6
Constitution and Committees 41

CHAPTER 7
The Secretaries, Professionals and Other Staff 43

CHAPTER 8
The War Years 1939 - 45 58

CHAPTER 9
Characters over the years 60

CHAPTER 10
The Ladies 74

CHAPTER 11
Suggestion Book 85

CHAPTER 12
The Gresham and Limpsfield Chart Golf Clubs 91

CHAPTER 13
Tandridge Today 93

APPENDIX 1
The Presidents, Captains and Lady Captains 108

APPENDIX 2
My Early Days at Tandridge by Alec Baker 114

Preface

My first thanks are due to the late Tony Englefield who in the last years of his life went to a great deal of trouble to produce his draft history of Tandridge over its first 60 years. I have made much use of his material throughout this book, especially in the early chapters.

I must also thank Ken Donegan who kindly provided nearly all the photographs included in the colour supplement and on the cover. I am grateful to Elizabeth Yule for her help in the preparation of the chapter on the Ladies; to Alec Baker for contributing Appendix 2; to Philip Truett for the provision of photocopies; and to John Berry, Duncan Ferguson, Selwyn Kennard and my wife, all of whom read the manuscript and made several useful improvements or corrections.

Finally there are the countless number of other people who in one way or another have assisted in the production of this book, whether by raiding their memories or by digging out old photographs. Without their help the job would have been much harder.

I hope the book will serve as a reminder of the good times we have all enjoyed - and continue to enjoy - as members of Tandridge Golf Club.

JOHN WILSON

May 1999

Leslie T Bailey

John Berry

Forewords

This book will be of great interest not only to members of Tandridge Golf Club but also to the many visitors and friends who have played our course.

We members owe a tremendous debt of gratitude to Tony Englefield and John Wilson for their meticulous research in collating this history celebrating our first 75 years. The result of their efforts illuminates the past for us in a most entertaining way and the names on the Honours Boards come to mean much more.

I have been a member since 1964 and yet had no real knowledge of the background to the Club's formation or of the distinguished past members and personalities who helped to create its character and reputatation.

The members of Tandridge Golf Club have been fortunate indeed to enjoy the foresight of our founder members who purchased the land, engaged an excellent course architect and laid down the structure and style which has served us so well. The basic character of the Club has been preserved making membership much sought after. We have a Club to be proud of and, as members, we are very aware of this.

Leslie Bailey
President

Our thanks must go to Tony Englefield and John Wilson who have both, at different times, done an enormous amount of work to produce this book.

In its 75th year Tandridge is a prosperous, thriving Club enjoyed and appreciated by members and visitors alike. Much of this is due to the vision, generosity and hard work done by many of the people described in this book. The Club has a rich history and I am sure you will enjoy reading it.

John Barr
Captain 1998-99

Chapter 1

Origin and Formation

The name "TENHRIC" first appeared around 965 AD and changed over the next century or so to "TENRIGA" (Domesday Book). Then "TENDRIGGA" became "TANRUGGE" (1265) before becoming "TANDRIDGE". The origin seems to be unknown, but is said to "derive from Saxon words of similar type, probably meaning ridges with swine pastures".

In the first quarter of this century, the regular golfers in the Oxted and Limpsfield area played on Limpsfield Chart golf course, as often as possible, but the limitation of 9 holes (even though tees varied for each 9) did not provide the full test of an 18 holes course which they sought.

Furthermore, no golf there was allowed on Sundays since the public common had to be available, as it now is, for walkers, picnickers, even cricketers - but hopefully not on the greens! Sunday morning golf only was not allowed until after the 1939-45 war.

Thus the idea was formulated in the early 1920's that an 18 holes golf course should be created somewhere in the vicinity which would undoubtedly have the enthusiastic support of a good number of locals.

Mr H S Colt, well known as an architect of golf courses, had been asked to inspect and consider possible sites around Limpsfield and Oxted. This included the wooded area between Limpsfield Chart church and Crockham Hill, the land to the north and east of the 5th hole at Limpsfield Chart (making that into an 18 hole course but with all the problems of no play on Sundays), and Tandridge Park. He, with an ad hoc Committee of Sir H J Gibson, G F Forwood, B A Cohen, A E Bell and Sir Ernest Clarke, agreed that the site on Tandridge Park estate seemed most suitable.

The search for alternative land from which a full 18 holes golf course could be created was greatly assisted by the favourable and generous reaction of Sir Bernard Greenwell, Bart. who owned a large acreage of land at Tandridge Park. Negotiations were opened, finance was considered, and in 1922 the whole project took shape in an embryonic way, as the following two letters demonstrate.

PROPOSED 18-HOLE GOLF COURSE AT TANDRIDGE.

Dear Sir,

A good 18-hole Golf Course is much needed in this neighbourhood.

Mr. Colt, the well known golf course architect, has recently been called in to inspect all likely ground in the vicinity, and on his advice a site on the Tandridge Park Estate has been selected as the most suitable, having a sandy soil and the other requisites for a really first class course.

The course adjoins the Oxted-Godstone Road, is about a mile from Oxted Station, and a motor bus service passes close to the proposed site of the Club House. The Course can be constructed at a reasonable cost, and if the work is started forthwith, the architect expects that a portion of the course could be available for play next summer.

The owner of the land, Sir Bernard Greenwell, Bart, of Marden Park, Woldingham, is prepared to grant a lease for 21 years, with option of purchase at any time during the currency of the lease, on terms that are considered favourable.

A sum of about £10,000 is required to cover the initial cost of laying out the course and the erection of a Club House. For this purpose guarantors of sums of *not less* than £100 each are asked for. A considerable portion of the total sum required has already been so guaranteed by residents of Oxted and Limpsfield, and it is necessary that the balance should be guaranteed at the earliest possible date, so that the scheme may be proceeded with forthwith. There is every reason to believe that the club will prove a success, as there should be no difficulty in obtaining the necessary number of members from the surrounding neighbourhood and elsewhere. It is proposed that guarantors of £100 and upwards should be elected to the club without entrance fee.

The Bank will be asked to advance the necessary funds to proceed with the work on the security of the guarantors, who will not be required to put up money until bonds are issued in lieu. A meeting of guarantors will be held as soon as possible, to settle the form of bonds and appoint a committee to frame rules, etc.

I shall be obliged if you will let me know at your earliest convenience whether you are prepared to be a guarantor for £100 or larger sum. A form is enclosed for this purpose.

Yours truly,

H. J. GIBSON,
(On behalf of the supporters).

WOODLANDS,
    OXTED.
November 2nd, 1922.

P.S.—The scheme is supported amongst others by:

RT. HON. SIR L. WORTHINGTON EVANS, G.B.E.,
    Doghurst, Limpsfield.
SIR E. CLARKE, Longacre, Oxted.
B. A. COHEN, K.C., Champions, Limpsfield.
SIR H. J. GIBSON, K.C.B., Woodlands, Oxted.
H. D. G. LEVESON GOWER, Hookwood, Limpsfield.
C. LEVESON GOWER, Hookwood, Limpsfield.
G. F. FORWOOD, West Chart, Limpsfield.
H. GIBSON, Inglenook, Limpsfield.
A. E. BELL, Lynwood, Limpsfield.
W. P. METCALFE, Stonehall, Oxted.

Proposed Tandridge Golf Club.

WOODLANDS,
OXTED,
SURREY,

December 23rd, 1922.

DEAR SIR OR MADAM,

Since the issue of my circular of November 2nd, negotiations have been practically completed for the acquisition of the land on the Tandridge Park Estate for an 18-hole Golf Course. SIR BERNARD GREENWELL, BART., the owner, has agreed to sell the necessary land on very favourable terms, on condition that it is restricted to golf. Under these conditions, for the first seven years the whole of the purchase money will be on mortgage at an exceptionally low rate of interest, while, if the Club desire it, for a further period of five years (making twelve in all) two-thirds will remain on mortgage at five per cent. interest.

The Provisional Committee consider these terms most attractive, and strongly recommend their acceptance.

It is estimated that fully £12,000 will be required for the construction of the golf course and the provision of a club house, and other necessary buildings. So far, promises have been received to take up bonds to an amount of approximately £7,000.

The Provisional Committee consider it would be unwise to proceed with the full scheme until at least £10,000 is guaranteed.

In the case of those who have already signed guarantees, no further action need be taken until they are called upon to sign the agreement to take a bond, which can be done either at the meeting on the 9th proximo, or before, by returning to me the form attached to the bond, with their signature and a sixpenny stamp affixed. Those who have not already signed guarantees should apply to me for bonds, stating the number required. Those applying before the 9th proximo will be entitled to attend the meeting.

A Meeting of Guarantors will be held at the HOSKINS ARMS HOTEL, on TUESDAY, JANUARY 9TH, 1923, at 6.15 p.m. (at which your attendance is earnestly requested), to confirm terms of purchase as detailed above, to approve form of Bond (copy enclosed), and to elect Committee.

Sketch Plans of the outlay of the Course as recommended by MR. COLT, will be available at Lloyds Bank, Oxted, on and after January 1st next.

Yours faithfully,

H. J. GIBSON.

Apart from the foresight and enthusiastic encouragement from George F. Forwood, the leading lights in this venture were Sir Henry Gibson, KCB. and Benjamin A Cohen, KC. Sir Henry Gibson was honoured as a senior Civil Servant. B A Cohen had practised at the Bar for many years before taking Silk in 1913 and becoming Legal Advisor to the Board of Trade during the 1914/18 War. After the war he sat as an Official Arbitrator and spent some years preparing a report to the Government on National Insurance. For this excellent service he was given a knighthood in 1929.

B A Cohen KC

These three were very ably and enthusiastically supported by A E Bell, Sir Ernest Clarke, and C E G Leveson Gower ("Clem") - all distinguished men, who were also keen golfers.

On 9th January 1923 a General Meeting was held at the Hoskins Arms, Oxted, the Chair being taken by B A Cohen KC. About 45 people were present to discuss the outline plans to buy land, form a Committee, and work out financial aspects.

Sir Bernard Greenwell, Bart. was evidently generous minded and sympathetic to the project, and negotiations began for the purchase of "146.344 acres on the north side of the wood known as

Windmillstadle Wood, with cottage and buildings erected thereon, and Furzefield Plantation ..... for the sum of £8,550".

Detailed discussions followed for the land purchase until exchange of contracts for sale and purchase on 7th November 1923, when the Club was represented by A E Bell, Sir Ernest Clarke, B A Cohen KC., and C E G Leveson-Gower. The contract referred to a tenant (Mr. Hopkins) who was farming 8.75 acres and vacant possession of that acreage was guaranteed by the Vendor. The generous nature of the deal was evidenced by the Vendor granting a mortgage of £8,592 (the purchase price being £8,550 so that certain expenses could be included), and the rate of interest was put at 2% for the first 5 years, then 3% for 2 more years and, at the borrower's option, a further 5 years at 5% interest on the loan outstanding. The Vendor reserved rights of pre-emption in case the Purchaser should wish to sell, and he also undertook to remove the cricket pavilion on the property (near the present site of the fourth green, but then overlooking the cricket pitch which was in the area in front of the seventh tee).

The Vendor covenanted not to use any of his adjoining lands (probably several hundred acres) for the purposes of a golf club or course, but "so that this (1) should not apply to land more than 5 miles from the Club House, (2) should cease if the members of the Club refused to take in suitable and proper members".

Following the first Committee meeting in January 1923 monthly meetings took place to discuss progress and make early decisions. Apart from persons already named, members elected to the Committee included A C Hamilton, C J de Rougemont, and J Grant Forbes. Mr A C Hamilton was appointed the first Secretary at £350 p.a. and was to live in the house on the course (The Pheasantry).

Bonds to be issued at £100 each, with certain rights, had been subscribed for up to a total of £4,700, and Mr Forwood instructed Mr Colt to prepare a plan for construction of the course at a cost not to exceed £6,000.

An estimate for £4,584 from John I Williams to construct the clubhouses was accepted on 17 November 1923. Plans for the construction of the two staff cottages at a cost not to exceed £1,000 for both were approved a few months later.

By November 1923 a report was received giving an estimate of £15,835 for construction of the course and buildings and legal formalities ensued to obtain possession of the cottage. Five men were hired to start work on the course layout under the direction of

Messrs Frank Harris of Guildford. Only £14,300 had then been received by the sale of Bonds but as the project progressed more subscriptions came along.

GOLFING February 1923

A NEW course is being laid out at Oxted, Surrey, in close proximity to Limpsfield Chart. Franks, Harris & Co., Guildford, are constructing.

GOLF MONTHLY December 1923

Tandridge Park, Surrey, the home of the Earls of Cottenham, has been purchased by a number of residents of Limpsfield and Oxted, with a view to the construction of a golf course.

Two newspaper cuttings in 1923

The first Hon. Auditor was L R Sankey. He was appointed Honorary Auditor by the Committee on 8th August 1924, but could only have carried out two audits as he was elected to the Committee at the 2nd Annual General Meeting on 28th November 1925. Another member, Donovan F E Whitehouse, who had his own firm, then took on the audit at a nominal fee of 10 guineas until the Club was on its feet when his firm was paid the then going rate. A considerable debt was, and is, owed by the Club to Mr Sankey, as will appear later.

The Bondholders were circularised to give notice that the course would be fully open on 1st October 1924, which presumably should be taken as the official opening date of the Club, although strangely the conveyance was not finally completed until June 1925.

Sir Bernard Greenwell was invited to become a free life member of the Club as some recognition of his great generosity. He was also nominated to be the Club's first President and although he was requested to accept, he declined so long as the mortgage continued.

However, at the First General Meeting, held on 21 February 1925, these appointments were made:

President	Sir Bernard F Greenwell, Bart
Vice Presidents	Sir Henry Gibson
	Rt Hon Sir L Worthington-Evans
Captain	B A Cohen K.C.
Members' Secretary	A C Hamilton
Architect:	H S Colt

The Committee recommended electing 70 men members and 20 lady members. The Ladies formed their own Committee of Mrs. Forwood, Miss Steward and Mrs Leach, with power to co-opt.

The original entrance fee for men members was fixed at 10 guineas, and the annual subscription 8 guineas.

At this date, 186 Bonds had been issued, with 14 being held at the option of Sir Bernard Greenwell. A budget of £4,000 p.a. to run the Club was assessed, but as subscriptions were only £2,270 a further 100 members were needed.

An EGM was held on 25 April 1925 at which it was agreed to accept 5 Day members at £5.5.0 entrance fee and £5.5.0 annual subscription.

On 4th July 1925 a further EGM was called to consider the difficult financial position - £3,000 in debts, and £1,500 was needed to carry on until September. The reasons for this situation were that 14 bonds had not been taken up, there had been a delay in opening the clubhouse, and members had not been joining as fast as anticipated. After a discussion, it was resolved to form a limited liability company with £15,000 capital, provided by 600 shares at £25 each. The proceeds would pay off the mortgage, discharge current liabilities, and leave a balance of £3,400. The Chairman and Sir Ernest Clarke urged the members to support the scheme and "save the course". Voting was 102 for and 10 against.

In September, yet another EGM was held to discuss the financial position, and eventually it was decided not to pursue the idea of forming a limited company. Various loans and gifts totalling £4,675 had meanwhile been provided by individuals and the finances were thus secured so that the Club was safe until 1926.

By October a letter had been received from Sir Bernard Greenwell's solicitor stating he was willing to waive one year's

TANDRIDGE GOLF CLUB.

September 4th, 1925.

DEAR SIR (OR MADAM),

It is understood that many members are reluctant to assist the Club until a meeting has been called to discuss certain suggested schemes, and the poor response to the Committee's latest appeal makes it evident that this is the case. **The Committee, therefore, give notice that an Extraordinary General Meeting of the Club will be held at the Club House, on Friday, September 25th, 8.30 p.m., for this purpose.**

In the meantime, the Committee desire to make the following observations :

Only three schemes have been presented to them ; two involve the formation of a Company, which is evidently not acceptable to members, and the third consists of a levy on the Bondholders, which seems not only impracticable, but unjust and unlikely to yield the necessary results.

It was clearly explained at the last meeting that if funds could not be raised for the purchase of the land, the only satisfactory alternative was a voluntary loan, and the sum required was estimated at approximately £5,000. Guarantors to the amount of £2,450 immediately came forward, and the Committee tender their heartiest thanks to these members and the few others who have agreed to assist the Club. Many of the guarantors have already sent cheques in liquidation of their guarantees or for larger amounts, and it is hoped that the other guarantors will follow the same course. If a further sum of £2,500 were subscribed by the rest of the members, the situation would be saved.

The course is in excellent condition ; visitors who are coming in increasing numbers are delighted with it, and many of them have expressed their desire to join. The Committee have arranged a professional exhibition match on October 17th, in which Braid, Ray, Mitchell and Baker will take part. Other matches amongst amateurs and Press Clubs are in course of arrangement, with a view to making the club better known. If members are unwilling to make the small sacrifice required of them, the trustees cannot complete the purchase and mortgage agreements. Moreover, the Committee consider it is unfair to accept the subscriptions of new members (the one element necessary to the success of the Club).

The Committee most emphatically state that, in their opinion, the future of the Club will be seriously endangered and possibly wrecked, unless the necessary support is forthcoming at an early date.

The Committee, including the Trustees, feel that the poor response to their appeal may possibly be due, in the case of some members, to a lack of confidence in themselves, and are quite willing to resign and hand over the management of the Club and trusteeship to others, if this is the wish of the members.

By order of the Committee,

A. C. HAMILTON,
Secretary.

interest on his mortgage. This generous act provided yet further relief at a difficult time.

Alfred Baker (nominated to be first Professional) was asked to stay on at Limpsfield Chart golf course for three months and, if he wanted to, to go to some first class Club to gain experience before taking up his duties at Tandridge. He was given £10 to enable him to visit Sunningdale (provided he accounted for this later). The Secretary noted in the minutes subsequently that "there was a balance due from A. R. Baker after paying his expenses".

The first Stewards, Mr and Mrs Barrett, were taken on jointly at £6.10 per month, and this was later increased to £100 p.a. with "all found". A Manageress (Miss Hunt) to organise catering was appointed at £90 p.a. and her assistant (Miss Ramsey) was engaged at £35 p.a..

Green Fees for visitors were fixed at 5/- per day.

The cottages (at the club entrance) were very small and G. MacDonald (first Greenkeeper) was authorised to have the use of the second cottage at a rental of 7/6d per week "provided the club should retain the use of one bedroom".

The first caddie master, C.J. Millen, was paid £2.15.0 per week- £2.10.0 as caddie master and 5/- for work outside the clubhouse. He had been the physical training instructor at Pilgrim's School, Westerham, where the Secretary had been Headmaster. The Secretary was authorised to purchase a football for the caddies.

An interesting request was made to the local bus company (East Surrey) suggesting that to assist golfers travelling to the club, the bus fare from Limpsfield Common to the club entrance should be reduced from 4 pence to 3 pence.

To assist the finances the provision of a bar was discussed with a Miss Hunt and in due course a rather cautious "hatch" at the end of the lounge was built. Drinks had to be ordered and taken through the hatch so that no unseemly bar paraphernalia was seen.

In the meantime, other events had taken place in 1925. On 4 April, the first match of the Club v. House of Commons (including R Boothby and Lord Brabazon) took place - the Club to pay for luncheon, the Committee to elect a team. Tandridge won 12 - 6.

Caddies had their fees increased to 1/10d (2nd class) and 2/4d (1st class).

On 25 May, an application from Rosslyn Park F.C. to play at the Club was not granted. No reason was specified........

In July Mr and Mrs Lloyd presented the Lloyd Cup for a competition match play knock out tournament to start in Autumn annually.

The Saunders Putter (an ebony and silver challenge putter) had been donated to the club by friends of the late S.G. Saunders. Silver discs were to be attached denoting the annual winner. This trophy is now housed in a glass case on the wall in the lounge. The competition was to be an 18 holes medal round, the best 8 scores leading to a play off in knockout match play to establish the winner.

By 1926 the Club was running along smoothly, and in February limits were set for members - Men 350 and Ladies 150.

Sir Ernest Clarke donated the Clarke Challenge Cup to be played for in the Spring and Autumn, entrance fees to be given to the local hospital (Oxted and Limpsfield). He also suggested that an annual fixture be made to play the Gresham Club from Limpsfield Chart G C. This match continues to this day.

In 1928 the sudden death of the Secretary (A C Hamilton) required temporary support, willingly given, from Sir E Clarke and L R Sankey, pending the appointment of a new Secretary - Lt Col J H Alexander.

In February 1932, W Allen was appointed Greenkeeper (in place of G MacDonald) at the then going rate of £4 p.w. and cottage.

A part repayment of £4,592 was made to reduce the mortgage in January 1930, and there followed a series of payments of £1,000 until the final redemption and discharge on 19th November 1932. The repayment of unsecured loans then ensued until the final conclusion in September 1935, but Bondholders who retained their Bonds were informed by the Committee that their interests had not been overlooked and it was hoped - subject to provisos - to pay interest on the Bonds by the end of 1938.

The privileges to which Bondholders were (and still are) entitled, such as reduced subscription and entrance fees, the right both to introduce guests without paying a green fee and to nominate the purchaser of one's house as a prority candidate for membership, were costing the Club about 4% p.a. on the Bonds in 1938. The cost remains not inconsiderable, but Bonds are now bought in by the Club whenever possible, either on the death of a member or if surrendered.

Chapter 2

The Fire

On 13 May 1927 (Friday the 13th) the whole Clubhouse was destroyed with all contents, following a fire which may have been started somewhere near the kitchen area. Owing to the thatched roof and no extinguishing apparatus, the fire spread quickly causing total destruction, except in the men's lavatory where certain china items remained still standing, rather rudely and prominently in evidence when all the dust had settled.

In the serious situation which followed, the Secretary had to retrieve the few papers he had in his desk which had been wisely moved out smartly on to the car park and he started preparing an insurance claim working from his own home. Most of the original records of the Club were reduced to ashes.

The "Times" gave a short summary of the event : "Clubhouse destroyed (opened 3 years ago). After 2 p.m. Morris (ground staff) saw smoke issuing from the thatched roof over the kitchen and gave the alarm. The members who were at luncheon went to assist by removing some items of furniture and effects. By the time the Oxted Fire Brigade appeared on the scene the whole building was a mass of flames and was destroyed in 1 1/2 hours. Only the brick chimneys and the gentlemen's urinals were left standing".

Bert Morris - more about him in the next chapter - had vivid recollection of the fire. He had been working on the putting green just outside the club lounge windows about mid-day, when he noticed a puff of smoke near the kitchen chimney, and then a flicker of flame. Dropping his tools he ran to the window to call Mrs Brown (the Manageress), or Ivy Harries or Queenie, who were kitchen helps. There was evidently some problem opening the windows to the lounge, but Mr Grammond (Captain 1938) jumped up from his armchair and quickly warned everyone around that a fire was blazing.

Bert told the Captain that he must go to the Secretary's office to get the safe out, because he assumed it would have money or valuables in it. The safe was somehow quickly manhandled out on to the lawn, and his desk and books were rushed out. The Secretary then arrived to assist last minute salvage, but little could be removed as the fire and smoke were too fierce. Seeing his safe on the lawn he turned to Bert and said "Who brought this out? There's nothing in it!" So Bert asked where the cash was kept, and Mr Hamilton replied, "Why, in my desk drawer of course" And, indeed, that's where it was - luckily!

Mrs Brown flapped around looking for her cat and shouted that she must rush upstairs to save him. This she attempted to do before the smoke and flames, which by then had become a fearsome sight, engulfed the whole scene. Her tears of sorrow at having to leave empty handed later turned to a different emotion when she discovered her cat sitting on the flower bed cleaning its paws and contemplating the panic with the quiet aplomb that only a cat can show with disdain for the human race.

During the pandemonium someone had called the local Fire Brigade whose equipment then consisted of a handcart (as a fire engine) containing some reels of hose and some buckets. About six men arrived, pulling the handcart up the hill from Oxted, and hastily unrolled the lengths of hose, joining them at each length, until the Club house was reached. The nearest hydrant was in the road at the drive entrance, and Bert recounted how the leading fireman connected the hose to the hydrant, switched on to test it, and filled his boots with water! By the time the water could be used the building had almost burned down - in under two hours.

All that remained of the clubhouse

The clubhouse was literally burnt out, the lead pipes fell out of the roof, the gutters caved in, and only the solid oak blocks in the lounge floor remained somewhat usable since, although charred and swollen, their durability had survived the whole incident. Charlie Coomber, the groundsman, suffered a blow on the head from a falling gutter whilst he had been trying to get some furniture out of the large windows. There was virtually a total loss, and this less than three years after the Club opened.

The origins of the fire were never clearly defined, but it is thought there was a dirty flue and some sparks from the kitchen fire may have caused an unseen glow which grew into heated embers and eventually erupted. The thatched roof and timber-framed building were a natural situation for a huge conflagration. The ashes from the fire flew on the wind down the 17th and 18th fairways, and floated on to the 13th and even as far as Tandridge Village.

After the fire, two temporary sheds were put up in the car park and these served as the clubhouse during the reconstruction period. These were surplus army huts; one was used as changing rooms, and the other as bar and dining room. The remains of the former was still there until quite recently. One side had been removed and was used as a garage for cars belonging to members of the staff.

Alf Baker had been playing on the 12th green when he saw the smoke from the fire and he rushed back to check his shop and stock. On arrival he found the firemen hosing the shop and enthusiastic helpers throwing clubs, bags, clothing, balls etc onto the ground outside causing some damage to them. He protested that these items could have been left to burn as they were all insured!

The urgency of the matter gave rise to quick settlement and the insurance claim was agreed on 27th June - "Clubhouse £6,400; Contents £930". These substantial figures were achieved thanks to the timely increase in cover made by the Committee on 27th March 1927 on the recommendation of L.R. Sankey.

A Special Committee was appointed to deal with all aspects of clearance, new building, temporary accommodation, etc and somehow business went on - if not quite as normal!

The new Clubhouse was built by John L Williams & Sons (Architect J Douglas Robinson) and was opened on 2nd February 1928, less than eight months after the fire. It was decided not to repeat the thatched roof which had been a feature of the previous building.

An alternative version

The Southwark Clergy were playing on the course that day, and their history (by their then Hon. Secretary, K G Hoare) gives a different version of the events leading up to the fire:

> "When the Club was founded, a very elaborate and costly clubroom was built, for lounge, bar & dining room combined. The offices and dressing rooms were hopelessly inadequate. Moreover the roof was thatched. From the very first members and visitors, I among them, said the only thing to do was to burn it down. So plans were set in motion. Insurance was raised to fabulous heights. Some ex-Army huts were purchased and erected alongside. When all was ready, Southwark Clergy arrived for their day's golf. Under this cloak of respectability, a match was put to the roof. As this went up in flames, the clergy came to the rescue from every jungle on the course, carried out all the valuable fittings and furniture into the waiting huts, and then continued their game. A grateful Club collected the insurance and erected the present palatial clubhouse, and have ever since felt compelled to treat us with the utmost generosity - hush money or spiritual blackmail!! "

Whether this is a true story remains a speculation, but a favourable cash settlement was clearly achieved.

Postscript - Another fire and a lucky escape

On Thursday 20th May 1999, Chris Evans (the new Professional) went out from his flat at about 11.15 pm to exercise his dog. He noticed smoke emanating from the back of the clubhouse and sensed something was wrong. He rang the fire brigade, and raised Percy Francis who opened up the back door. They discovered that a blaze had started in the laundry room - due to an electrical fault in one of the machines located there. The paintwork and walls were already alight.

The fire brigade arrived within five minutes, accompanied by two police cars. The fire was quickly extinguished but not before the dense smoke and fumes had caused £30,000 of damage throughout the kitchen area and the Gallery Bar. The massive clean up operation, left to experts called in by the insurers, was only just completed in time for the 75th celebration dinner.

As one of the firemen said, "Another five minutes, and you would not have had much of a clubhouse left......."

Chapter 3

Bert Morris

One of the most interesting characters concerned with the origins of the course was Bert Morris. His portrait in oils showing "Albert Morris 1924-75" is in the lounge. He, with the first Head Greenkeeper, W Allen, was responsible for much of the basic layout and physical construction of the course in 1923 when the course architect's plans had to be put into action with Harris Brothers (contractors).

The course was opened in September 1924 after about 12 months preparation of digging, mowing, tree lopping, shrub removal, grass sowing, turf laying and incessant trimming, cutting, and then mowing, mowing, mowing ..... Horses were used for much of the work but hand labour was the main method employed.

Bert Morris - by Johnny Jonas

The 10th fairway between the road and the green had to be cut through the wood as the wood on the right and that on the left were joined together. Graham Sankey remembers seeing the stumps being pulled out by a tractor. A hawser was attached to each stump in turn and the tractor accelerated to full speed. The stump did not always come out first time: how the driver avoided breaking his neck on each occasion remains a mystery.

The large number of bunkers (some say originally one for each day of the year) was one of the architect's instruments of torture, and the preparation of each one needed considerable labour in the digging, base formation, sand filling and bank construction according to the lay of the land. Bert was always out on the course with his horses, machinery, and a staff of several men dealing with the heavy construction work in all weathers, but his pride in his work carried him along and, even at the age of 84, he glowed when one recalled the importance of his presence at the birth of the course.

Bert was involved with Tandridge from the age of 18 (starting salary 13 shillings per week) and worked on the course until he was 68. When the 13th fairway was prepared the field of hay on the right had to be mown, and the clubhouse could be clearly seen across the valley of the 14th. The numerous trees now filling the right of the 13th and making such a steep and perilous area for the sliced drive, have grown up over the intervening years.

The cricket pitch originally in front of the 7th tee had served the local cricket team for many years, and the excellent turf can still be seen in the rough at the start of the 7th fairway. The cricket pavilion had been situated near the 4th green and the Vendor of the land agreed to have this removed during the first 12 months after the sale. The fir trees to the right of the beginning of the 7th hole were planted by Bert and his team.

If Bert found a good golf ball during his work, he would clean it up and sell it to Alf Baker for 9 (old) pence. He remembers "young Alec" and "even younger Ron", who could play equally well left or right-handed.

Bert, with a handicap of 8, remembers a wonderful round (unauthenticated) he had in 1929 when he beat Alf Baker 6 and 4. This, he said, was during the Hamilton Cup. With the prize money, £3 and 15 shillings, he bought a new bicycle.

Some areas of the course had special names in the early days - such as the 18th fairway ("windy ridge"), 1st and 9th ("stormy park"), 2nd, 3rd and 4th ("Tandridge Park"), 14th and 17th ("Little Horror") and so on. This helped the men to know which areas were being referred to during course preparation.

Bert asserted that with another man he had originally "stepped out" the whole length of the course from tee to green, all the way round and had arrived at a total of 8,400 yards. Later more exact measurements by chain etc. established the yardage on the card.

Caddying one day for a Mr Taylor, he remembered that the 9th hole was completed in 2 shots with a No. 1 iron and a No. 4 holed out. He also saw Peter Alliss drive the 16th green from the back tee - over the fir tree. This has been done subsequently by various long hitters.

The late Philip Jonas one day had Bert as his caddy. On the 2nd hole, Bert selected a 4 iron for his second shot. Philip, who had enjoyed a good lunch and a glass or so of port, said "I can see 3 balls, which shall I hit?". Bert replied "Hit the middle one". Phil promptly put his ball on the green, six inches from the pin.

A member, Woolf Barnato, whose racing drive prowess at Brooklands Racetrack was well-known, used to tear up the drive in his Bentley, or other racing car, blowing his horn with some vigour to attract the caddies' attention and ensure that his golf bag was prepared for use. This extrovert personality often brightened the scene with his numerous glamorous girl friends who looked equally attractive in his sports car or walking the course.

Bert remembers a visiting mongrel dog which used to meander in through the entrance gate and wander along the 1st fairway and rough at any time of day. This dog had a propensity to pick up golf balls and chew them or run off with them. Once Bert had spotted this habit, he decided to plaster a couple of balls with mustard, and so, it seems the bait was taken and the trouble cured!

Bert referred to Miss Minoprio as the first lady to play golf in trousers at Tandridge - about 1930. He also mentioned Neil Simmonds and his course record of 64, but this was before the 14th tee was put back to its present position.

In 1930 the greens were afflicted with long growing clonal bents in the grass and all eighteen greens had to be moved to temporary sites for many months to allow fresh turf to be laid and thoroughly established. As most greenkeepers train at Bingley, Yorks, the expression "Yorkshire fog" became a common expression to refer to patches of green and brown weed mixture which sometimes defaced the putting surfaces.

Work started early in the old days. Bert had to get up and out on the course by 4 a.m. in high summer in order to water certain distant greens, where the water pressure was insufficient during the day. On one occasion he was stopped by a police constable at the entrance as his tools and bag seemed suspicious. To allay the law representative's worry he offered to walk with him, and they went together to the 11th tee where the water was duly turned on and watering started.

In the 1920's there were six groundsmen and each was responsible for three greens. This was to ensure continuity - and pride - in the work, so any problems could be pin-pointed and responsibility was clearly fixed. The system may have been repetitive but, apparently, there was competition to achieve the best results - "a pride in one's work". In total there were sixteen greenkeepers, the others being two bunker rakers, two mechanics in the workshop, five others for tees etc plus the Head Greenkeeper.

Chapter 4

The Course

The course was designed by Mr H S Colt, and is regarded as being an excellent example of his style of architecture.

Mr Colt's architecture and layout of the course has been carried out on a "grand, bold scale, eminently fair, but devilishly ingenious" (The Times).

"Glorious views to the west and north, the downs from Reigate Hill to the west, to Caterham, Titsey Wood and Westerham Hill. To the south lies Crowborough Beacon, Ashdown Forest, and St. Leonards Forest. The soil is sandy, with excellent drainage, providing reasonable play even in wet weather. It is a fair sporting course for "tigers" and not too difficult for modest performers" (Surrey Mirror).

Bernard Darwin wrote the following in a pamphlet on the course, published in 1925.

"I think the first impression which the stranger gains of Tandridge is one of bigness and boldness. This is produced by its surroundings as well as by the course itself. The course stands high and enjoys a noble expanse of view. On the one side is the edge of the North Downs, a big semicircle of chalk hills, and on the other we may, on a fine day, see over the blue undulating distance as far as Crowborough and Ashdown Forest. It is a view on a grand scale and the course seems to be trying, very successfully, to live up to it. More especially in the second nine holes the hills and valleys are bold and sweeping, and there are shots to be hit from high places, which must quicken the most sluggish pulse. And then many of the bunkers have a really superb air. They are big enough and bold enough for anything, and involve sometimes a very deep drop into perdition. Mr Colt was the architect, and his bunkers and the greens guarded by them always look proud and defiant, which is as characteristic as it is picturesque. He is extraordinarily skilful in building up a plateau green so that it appears to have been made by the hand of Nature. At Tandridge he has at two holes done something still more skilful in building a long narrow gorge leading up to the green, and flanked by

Early pictures of the course, showing (above) the lack of surrounding trees and (below) the spindly fir trees that used to form a background to the 13th green.

cavernous bunkers, which looks as romantic as it does formidable........

"The course is roughly in the shape of a figure eight with its two loops apiece each beginning and ending at the clubhouse. This is today the fashionable shape for a golf course, but it has much more than fashion to recommend it, since it doubles the starting places and practically halves the number of players. And with that let us start out and play the first hole, an excellent type of opening hole, long enough to get the players well away and not so severe as to discourage or delay them. It is a good hole, moreover (440 yards long), for it wants two full shots, and there are bunkers both to right and left, especially to the left where stands a whole phalanx of them at various intervals.

"The second, again, wants two very full shots if we play it from the back tee. It is a little shorter than the first, but decidedly "dog-legged". A fringe of trees insists on one keeping well away to the left, and then turning half right we must hit our second up to a pretty terraced plateau tucked away in a corner. The third (380 yards) is straightforward and ordinary by comparison, but quite a good hole and the second shot must be an accurate one. It must also be in the air for there is one dominating bunker of strong character right in the middle of the course.

"Now we come to the first of the short holes, a seductive and also rather frightening one, for the green is narrow and the bunkers rage furiously together, those below it on the left being particularly deep and terrifying. It is a capital hole and eminently characteristic of Mr Colt at his best. Very attractive too is the fifth with another long narrow green heavily bunkered on either side, and a second shot to be played well out to the right on the line of a solitary silver birch so that may come swinging round to the hole.

"Now we turn back again - and I should have said earlier that we are contiually turning and tacking and so shall never get tired of any particular wind. The sixth wants a high and accurate iron shot for the second, over a diagonal line of bunkers; and at the seventh, if we hit a good tee shot, we may hope to be home with a pitch- and-run through a rather narrow opening to a gently rising green. The eighth is another short hole (160 yards) to a green with a picturesque background of Scots pines. There are some big bunkers to the left which present rather a magnetic appearance from the tee. It looks unpleasantly easy to get into them, just because it is so easy to hook a full iron shot, and this is exactly what one must not do.

Two other views from the early days. In the top photo, the 13th tee is very exposed with the clubhouse clearly visible above the bunkers around the 18th green. The photo below shows the absence of trees on the bank in front of the 18th green.

"Let us hope that we got a three at the hole because we are extremely likely to take five at the ninth. First we must hit a good drive to get clear of some woodland on our right, and next a very full second up one of those romantic gorges I mentioned before. The second is rather uphill, so that the hole will probably play longer than its 435 yards; altogether an uncommonly good four and quite a respectable and satisfactory five. That brings us back to the clubhouse and the turn and now we shall find ourseles in the more adventurous and mountainous country.

"Not for the first two holes, though both are quite interesting, especially the 10th, where the green is in a wooded corner and the second shot is over a line of bunkers set *en echelon*. With the twelfth the golf begins to be unquestionably dramatic. First comes a dog-legged tee shot round the corner of a wood, and then a second up another of Mr Colt's gorges to a green at the foot of a clump of Scots pines. There is a particularly lovely view from this green: there is also a particularly big bunker at the right-hand edge of the green which is very likely to catch us.

"Next comes an extraordinarily deceitful short hole. I took a mashie out of my bag to play it with a breeze behind me, and then looked at the card and found it over 200 yards long. The hole runs a little downhill, and there is quite a considerable stretch completely hidden from the tee in a fold in the ground. The green lies in something of a dip or pit, and there are bunkers everywhere, or so it seemed to me, except on the straight line to the hole and a big drop to destruction on the right. It is a capital hole, and the fourteenth is a fine one too of an eminently spectacular type. First comes an exhilarating tee shot from the height down to the valley, and then a full, a very full, brassey from the valley to the opposite height, crowned with bunkers. When the ground is slow this hole may be a little too long, but in summer, when even ordinary mortals can get home with driving irons, it must be glorious fun.

"The fifteenth is a comparatively commonplace short hole, though it calls for accuracy but the sixteenth is very entertaining - a good example of the "drive-and-a-pitch" hole, where the pitch must be a real pitch with no sneaking round or running up. I do not know how many bunkers surround the green, but they give the impression of a minefield.

"The seventeenth has another heartening tee shot from a pulpit, to be followed by an accurate iron shot to a plateau, well and truly guarded and at the last comes perhaps the best tee shot of all, where we go just as far right and cut off as big a hunk of hillside as we dare. The good and bold shot will gain its reward, for it alone can give us a

Alf Baker approaches the 14th green. Note the absence of the ditch across the fairway and the bunkers above the green.

chance of getting home: and even so our second must be of an arrow-like straightness along the top of a ridge. Altogether, it is a very fine hole and, when we do get there, we find a particularly good, keen green on which to hole our last putt. Bogey takes 76 for the round, and that is no mean score. To be sure he takes some fives where we may think we ought to do fours, but many of these fours at Tandridge want a good deal of getting."

Changes over the years

What changes have taken place in the past 75 years? Comparatively few, but the major ones are listed here - excluding the filling in of many bunkers (see "before and after" maps at the front and back of book). Dates are author's best guesses.

1st: New back tee built prewar. Bunker placed to front right of green c. 1960.

2nd: Tee moved to left of 1st green in 1931 after complaints from the AA that one of their patrols had been put in danger by someone driving down the A25. Tee restored to its original site in 1963 when trees had grown up and with a new wire mesh fence. Trees and bushes planted on right of fairway c. 1955. Bunker to left of green changed c. 1992.

3rd: Trees planted on right rough as hole moved more to the left, and green changed, all c. 1950. Bunkers in middle of fairway filled in c. 1960. Bunkers to right of green changed c. 1990.

4th: No changes.

5th: New back tee built pre-war. Bunkers on right of fairway changed c. 1990.

6th: Back tee lenghtened 1960. Wood to left of fairway planted c. 1955. Trees added to back of green c. 1952.

7th: Tee moved from between 4th green and 6th green to present site in 1933, after an accident. Grass bunker to right of fairway changed to "Bailey's copse" c. 1985. Bunkers to left of green changed c. 1992.

8th: Tee relaid c. 1993. New cross bunkers in middle of fairway put in c. 1970.

9th: New back tee created in 1953. Bunker created on right before road c. 1970 and changed c. 1992.

10th: Tee relaid c. 1993. Bunker between 10th and 18th hole removed c. 1990. Three trees planted between 10th and 18th fairway c. 1992. Tree on right hand grass bunker in fairway allowed to grow.

11th: Present ladies tee at the 11th hole was erected originally as a men's tee for use on Sunday mornings. In the days of one-car families and help in the home, a couple used to drive to the Club - father played golf and mother walked along the footpath to Tandridge Church. With a succession of ladies using the footpath at 30 yard intervals it was impossible for fourballs to use the proper tee. Bunker to right extended into fairway c. 1992. In 1935, Mr Colt was asked to redesign 11th and 12th to avoid crossing over, and did this by interchanging 12th tee and 11th green.

12th: New back tee built prewar. Trees planted up left hand side c. 1960 and 1995.

13th: New back tee built c. 1965. For a few years in the fifties or early sixties a shallow bunker was created at the back right of the green, which became known as "Siemssen's folly" as it was felt that to land in it was too harsh a penalty. Main tee renovated c. 1993.

14th: New back tee built c. 1965. The ditch across the fairway was laid when George Tweeddale was Captain in 1966.

15th: New tee laid c. 1992. Interesting hump in right hand side of green removed c. 1955.

16th: Rumour has it that - pre-war - the owner of the house adjoining the 16th tee had a dispute with the Club, over the boundary fence. He refused to allow the Club to move it and instead built a further extension to his house as near to the fence as possible! New back tee relaid c. 1970. Trees planted to left of fairway c. 1955. Ladies tee moved back c. 1980.

17th: Tees moved prewar from below 16th green to present position. During Arthur Cohen's time as Captain in 1952, he had it put back to the old position, but this did not last. The forward, pre-war tee is still used in the winter months. Bunker on right hand side of fairway removed c. 1955. Bunker in left rough removed c. 1986.

18th: Bunker installed on right hand side of hill c. 1952, but was later removed as being unfair. The fairway bunker between 18th and 10th hole was removed c. 1990.

The course has recently gained two elegant fountains of drinking water at the 6th and 14th tee respectively, given by the WOFFs (Wives out for fun) and John Cox. Duncan Ferguson kindly provided the warning bell now placed on the left of the second fairway.

The great storm in October 1987 caused tremendous damage on the course, with trees uprooted and flattened everyhere. As the Secretary (Tim Lloyd) said at the time, "in two hours we cleared woodland which would otherwise have taken us at least 10 years".

The Secretary managed to find two Yorkshiremen who spent some six months living on the course and clearing all the debris. The course itself was open again within a few days. The disappearance of some trees to the right of the 13th green opened up again the atttractive vista looking towards the clubhouse in the distance. An appeal was launched by the Club to raise funds to help pay for this unexpected occurrence.

John Bishop has worked at Tandridge since leaving school at the age of 15, and has been Head Greenkeeper for over 20 years. Greenkeeping has become much more technical and expensive in recent years, due to increased traffic on the course and the higher expectation of members. John has drawn much of his experience and knowledge from his predecessor Bert Fordham, and externally from agronomists Jim Arthur, David Stansfield and Neil Squires.

Although not long enough for a "Championship" course, Tandridge presents itself, elegantly and naturally clad in most seasons, as a challenge and an encouragement to the average golfer, and thought provoking to the less able player. The undulations require thought and skill to negotiate, and the borrows on the greens give constant problems, even for those who have played it many times.

The Practice Grounds

The area of land (3 acres, 3 roods and 27 perches) now used as the practice ground was originally part of the freehold of Sir Bernard Greenwell's estate. He died in 1939 but had imposed a covenant on that area to the effect that "no part should be used at any time for the purposes of a golf club or links". Mr. Cockburn (of the well known port family) had bought this land and the small house alongside the 16th tee which he converted into the present mansion. This is now owned and used by Canon UK who had purchased it from Midland Bank plc in the late 1980s.

On 18th October 1948 the practice ground was conveyed for £1,500 to the Midland Bank who released the covenant, and years later on 13th December 1960 sold the same land to F.G.E. Binns, a member of the Club. He being very well inclined to the Club made a most generous gift of the area to Tandridge by transfer in October 1961. Regrettably he died soon thereafter, and his generosity was slightly marred by the Inland Revenue's claim for estate duty since he had not survived the five year period for estate duty then needed for total clearance of such duty regarding "gifts inter vivos". Nonetheless the Club was greatly indebted to him.

In 1987 the Committee decided to spend £17,000 in creating the small additional practice ground for approach and bunker shots, on the left of the drive as the clubhouse is approached.

Chapter 5

The Clubhouse and Other Buildings

The original clubhouse

The Clubhouse was rebuilt after the fire (see Chapter 2) on the same site. The architect was a Mr Douglas Robinson who received a fee of 100 guineas plus his out of pocket expenses.

The dining room was added to the lounge in 1936. Prior to that time, meals were taken at tables in the lounge running the length of the room on the South side, under the balcony. The possibility of building a room over the dining room was discussed in 1988, but no action was taken. The internal ceiling was redesigned in the Spring of 1999.

The interior of the original clubhouse (compare with colour photo in supplement)

The new clubhouse, before the addition of the dining room or the Secretary's office

The Secretary's circular office was also built in 1936, replacing his old office which was at the end of the present Men's bar. The separate office for the Secretary himself was added in 1987.

The original clubhouse had only hatches and no bars until 1962 when, after several years' vocal campaigning by Bill Stow, Bill Igoe and others, the Committee agreed to a bar being built in the Men's bar. It was extended into the lounge a year or two later.

The Men's changing rooms extension was built in 1938. The major reconstruction of the ablutions area into their current design did not take place until 1995 at a cost of £27,000.

On 28 October 1967 the Committee gave the go ahead for the construction of the present Pro's shop and the three flats above. This valuable new building was completed in the following year.

The Ladies showers etc also underwent various changes, the most recent being in 1994.

After much deliberation - and considerable opposition from some of the older members - the gallery was extended and rebuilt to provide a mixed spike bar and a snack area in 1993. At the same time the doors leading to the outside balcony were refitted allowing the whole of the area outside to be used again. The Captain in the year when the main construction took place was Philip Warcup, who went to great lengths to ensure that its cost was kept within the budget of £80,000. The choice of furniture, carpet and decor was the work of Elizabeth Reynolds and Catherine Bailey. The Gallery Bar (as it is now called) has proved to be very popular with both members and visitors. Many people use it for lunches and other meals such as the enormous "Tandridge Breakfast".

The changes to the Gallery Bar meant that further alterations took place in what had been a steward's flat in the rooms behind, to provide further cooking facilities and a proper rest room for the staff.

The kitchens were completely modernised in 1996, and now comply fully with the relevant Health and Safety regulations.

Part of the Professional's accommodation was used in 1991 to make a common room in which the Junior members could meet. This room proved not to be used much by the Juniors and it reverted to being a further store room for electric trolleys in 1994. The Professional's shop itself was extended during Alec Baker's time and was completely refitted in 1998 after the arrival of Chris Evans.

The buildings used by the green staff have been improved at various times over the years, culminating with the construction of proper shower facilities and an office for the Head Greenkeeper in 1995.

Similar improvements to The Pheasantry have taken place from time to time. It now a very comfortable 4-bedroomed house complete with new double glazed windows throughout.

The Pheasantry in 1923 and as it is today

In 1987, Laporte Ltd applied to mine Fullers Earth in the fields on the other side of the lane running up the right hand side of the 3rd hole. Tandridge - led by senior trustee Jack Hamer - joined in the objections to this proposal, and after protracted hearings Laporte withdrew from the scene. In 1999, the Club were advised that 44 acres of this land were on the market at a guide price "in excess of £120,000" so the Committee decided not to pursue this.

The Club also turned down the chance to purchase 31 acres of the hilly, wooded land adjoining the 14th and 15th holes in 1988/89.

THE TANDRIDGE PROFESSIONALS
(From l. to r.) Michael Gibson, Chris Evans, David Green

THE TANDRIDGE GREENKEEPERS
(From l. to r.) John Crittell, Neil Burchett, Paul Bowen, Gary Bishop, John Bishop, Lee Thackaberry

Chapter 6

The Constitution and the Committee

In 1925 the Club had four Vice Presidents - Dr E P Andrae, Sir Henry Gibson, Charles Leweson-Gower and the Rt. Hon. Sir L Worthington-Evans Bt. . By 1946, Dr Andrae and Charles Leveson Gower were still in office plus Sir Ernest Clarke, but by 1974 when Dr Andrea was elevated to become President, no further appointments were made. However, in 1992, Leslie Bailey became a Vice President after his retirement as Hon. Treasurer for several years, and he continued in this role until he was elected President in 1997. There are now no Vice Presidents of the Club.

The Club's rules have always provided that the Committee should comprise the Captain, four Trustees and six ordinary members. The first Trustees were set out in the rules and were A E Bell, Sir E M Clarke, B A Cohen KC and C E G Leveson Gower.

Originally their appointment was until the next Annual General Meeting, but it seems clear that they continued in office until they resigned or died.

In the year 1945/46, the Annual report shows that the four Trustees had become H G Marshall, Geoffrey Heyworth (later Lord Heyworth), Walter Lines (of Triang toys fame) and A E M Gale. Walter Lines remained a Trustee for a further 16 years.

Kenneth Robinson became a Trustee in 1949 - the year he became Captain - and he too continued for a further 15 years. In more recent years, Roy Siemssen was elected a Trustee in 1962 and continued until 1984.

Undoubtedly the presence of the four Trustees has brought continuity to the Committee's deliberations.

A move, led by John Wilson when he was Senior Trustee in 1995, to change the constitution into a two tier structure was rejected by the Committee of that year.

In the first rules, it was also laid down that at each Meeting of the Club, the President, or in his absence, the Captain, should take the

Chair at all Meetings. At some stage this must have changed as in recent years the Captain has been Chairman at those Meetings.

In 1994, the rules regarding the winding up, dissolution or sale of the Club were strengthened. A resolution to that effect, or to sell a substantial part of any of the Club's assets, can now only be proposed at a General Meeting convened at not less than six weeks' notice. In order to be carried three-quarters of all members entitled to vote must vote in favour of the resolution.

At the same time, the Club's rules were changed to give the Ladies a vote at the AGM.

Chapter 7

The Secretaries, Professionals and Other Staff

In January 1923, the first Secretary was appointed. A C Hamilton acted most efficiently in the early days of establishing the administration and was rewarded with an annual salary of £350 and the use of "The Pheasantry", the pleasant house (formerly a small brick cottage, subsequently enlarged in 1925) near the 11th tee. The name derives from the former use of that area of Tandridge Park which was set up an a pheasant hatchery located near the present 17th green, to provide targets (and food) for the local sporting gentry.

A C Hamilton was Jean Hamilton's father and he ran the boys' school "Pilgrims" at Westerham before he took on the Club's affairs. His school masterly manner evidently kept the members almost in as much awe as his schoolboys. The Hamilton family moved into The Pheasantry in 1925. Jean was a pupil teacher at The Hill School, Westerham, and stayed there until August 1928 when A C Hamilton died suddenly whilst on holiday at the age of only 51. The basic rules and standards he laid down with quiet efficiency have continued and set a solid pattern for those who followed.

A C Hamilton

The interregnum was filled by senior Committee members until Col Alexander was appointed and moved into the house. The Colonel held office for 4 years, and was succeeded in 1933 by C N M Hamilton (no relation to the first Secretary). He was an electrical engineer working at one time in Hong Kong and came to England in 1917/18 but did not pass the medical to let him join the Armed Forces. He had been Secretary at Cooden Beach Golf Club and also at Betchworth Golf Club. His personal control of the Club's business included meticulous records, letters, and all usual formal details in his own handwriting.

Mr Hamilton's stay at The Pheasantry continued until 1956 when he died at the age of 57. During his illness which lasted for the major part of the year prior to his death the then Captain Roy Siemssen - with several members - devoted much personal time to running the Club.

Brigadier Giles succeeded C N M Hamilton but was a disaster and was "allowed to leave" within a year. Peter Knight was Captain at the time. Captain Godfrey Brewer DSO RN followed and brought his naval administrative experience to benefit the Club for many years with quiet efficiency and a delightful sense of humour. He retired in 1969 when Lieutenant Colonel Kenneth Evans took over.

The Colonel (Ken) put his own Army style on the job and ran things along very happily until his most untimely illness overcame his physical strength, and he passed away on 30th November 1982. Graham Sankey then acted unofficially as Secretary, assisted by Paul Burnett on the accounts and Peter Burles on the course, until Ken Evans' successor arrived in May 1983.

The Club then chose an RAF character, Air-Vice Marshal D C A (Tim) Lloyd, to take over the reins from his able naval and army predecessors. Tim's distinguished career ensured a most efficient and enthusiastic Secretary to the great benefit of the Club, and the multifarious details of organising members, committees, staff, societies, the course, the finances etc. were all ably and willingly taken in hand. His ready wit, merry quips and after dinner speaking were, and still are, renowned.

Tim Lloyd retired to Deal in 1989, and was succeeded by a distinguished amateur golfer, Ian Wheater. Unfortunately he was not so successful as an administrator and he left to join Berkhamsted Golf Club in December 1990.

He was followed by Major Adrian Furnival, who came to Tandridge after service with Wildernesse and Thorndon Park Golf Clubs. During his time with the Club he was involved in many changes, including new staff contracts of employment, the construction and opening of the Gallery Bar, the replacement of the Piggotts with a chef, and the receipt of the large VAT refund in 1994. He left in 1995 to become Manager of Windlesham Golf Club.

OBITUARIES
Capt Godfrey Brewer

CAPTAIN GODFREY BREWER, who has died aged 87, was one of the most distinguished and successful convoy escort captains of the 1939-45 War.

Leading the first Support Group in the sloop Pelican, Brewer took part in a fierce seven-day air and sea battle against the U-boats around Convoy ONS5 in May, 1943. Pelican herself sank U438, one of seven U-boats destroyed in and around that convoy — part of a total score of 42 U-boats that month.

Such appalling losses led to the temporary withdrawal of U-boats from the North Atlantic convoy routes, and for his part in the victory, which amounted to a strategic success comparable to Medway and Stalingrad, Brewer was awarded the DSO.

Godfrey Noel Brewer was born in 1900 and joined the Navy as a 13-year-old cadet in 1914, going to Osborne and Dartmouth. As a midshipman in the battleship Royal Sovereign he witnessed the surrender of the German High Seas Fleet in 1918 and its scuttling in Scapa Flow a year later.

After being sent for two terms to Cambridge University, Brewer wanted to become a specialist gunnery officer. But he also became engaged to be married, and the captain of the gunnery school, Whale Island, let it be known that marriage and gunnery were incompatible. So Brewer became a "salt horse" (destroyer officer), and never regretted it.

His first destroyer command was Whitehall on the China Station in 1934 and he went on to command the destroyer Vanquisher during the Abyssinian crisis of 1935 and the Veteran in the Spanish Civil War, when his coolness defused a dangerous diplomatic situation after the German pocket battleship Deutschland arrived off the Spanish port of San Sebastian in July 1936.

Brewer sent one of his officers across to the Deutschland to persuade the German Adml Carls not to land a large armed guard of 50 men. Carls later thanked Brewer for his advice.

At the outbreak of the 1939-45 War Brewer commanded the destroyer Maori and took part in the Norwegian campaign in 1940. But the strain of those operations, including the evacuation of Namsos under almost constant air attack, affected Brewer's health so that he had to give up the command of Maori. After sick leave he went in August 1940 to the Admiralty as Convoy Planning Officer in the Trade Division.

There his problems were exacerbated by the failure by the Admiralty and Downing Street to understand the traditional virtues of convoy. Most exasperating to Brewer and his colleagues were the suggestions of "Prof" Lindemann, Mr Churchill's scientific adviser, about whom Brewer would say: "I used to pray at nights that he would be run over by a bus."

In the summer of 1942 Brewer went back to sea, relieving the celebrated Capt "Johnny" Walker, in command of the 36th Escort Group in the sloop Stork. Stork was torpedoed and badly damaged during the "torch landings" in North Africa that year. The whiplash effect of the explosion which threw Brewer across Stork's bridge caused back injuries which plagued him all his life.

The next year Brewer was in the sloop Egret, commanding another escort group in the Bay of Biscay, when she was hit by a glider bomb and sank with great loss of life.

In 1944 he assumed his final wartime command in the new destroyer Caesar which took part in Arctic convoys before joining the Eastern Fleet in 1945. When the cruiser Cleopatra arrived in Trincomalee, Brewer signalled that after a lapse of 2,000 years Caesar intended to call on Cleopatra that evening. He was duly rowed across by his officers in a native craft, dressed in a makeshift toga and with a laurel wreath around his brow.

After the war Brewer was director of naval recruiting. His final appointment was as Captain of the Royal Naval College, Greenwich. After retirement he went out to New Zealand as a member of the New Zealand Navy Board.

Brewer was subsequently secretary of Tandridge Golf Club. His witty memoirs, The Melody Lingers On, appeared in instalments in the Naval Review in 1973-74. He leaves a wife, Joy, and one son.

Obituary for Capt GN Brewer RN, DSO

The four Secretaries (clockwise) are CNM Hamilton, Capt GN Brewer RN, DSO Lt Col KM Evans, and Air-Vice Marshall DCA Lloyd CB

A return to ex-service people followed with the appointment in 1995 of the present Secretary, Lieutenant Commander Selwyn Kennard, RN. His previous experience in the Navy - including being responsible at one time for the catering on HM Hermes for some 2,000 officers and other ranks - has proved to be invaluable in providing fresh leadership to the staff, both on the course and in the clubhouse. Very little escapes his eagle eyes.

Selwyn Kennard and "Pip"

The Professional and Assistants

The first "pro" Alfred Baker, known as Alf - came from Limpsfield, having been pre-selected by the Committee just before the construction of the course started. He had two sons - Alec and Ron.

In 1924 the cottages at the entrance to the course were occupied but eventually, when vacant possession was obtained, the Baker family moved in. Everything had to start from scratch, and prior to the shop being available for display of clubs and equipment, Alf sold golf balls from a suitcase - charging 2/6d for three balls. Emery cloth was used to clean clubs and a rather basic wooden hut served as the Pro's shop for some years.

CNM Hamilton and Alf Baker

Alf had a paternal and easy manner which served well for instruction, and his natural "no-nonsense" down-to-earth swing and steady temperament kept his scores consistently near to par for the course. His style based on the traditional older school contrasted somewhat with that of his two sons.

THE FIRST EXHIBITION MATCH
(From l. to r.) Alec Herd, Ted Ray, Alfred Baker and Harry Vardon

The first Exhibition match on 17th October 1925 was staged between famous golfers of the time, namely Harry Vardon and Alec Herd against Ted Ray and Alf. The morning round produced better ball scores of 71 on both sides, and in the afternoon Vardon and Herd put in 70 against 71, all this being reported in the "Surrey Mirror". The photograph in the main lounge (reproduced on previous page) provides a record of the historic event, and shows Alec Herd (Open Champion 1902), Ted Ray (Open Champion 1912, American Open Champion 1920), Alfred Baker (Tandridge Golf Club) and the famous Harry Vardon (Open Champion 1896-98-99, 1903-11-14 and American Open Champion 1900).

Alf died on 6 December 1949, but had retired earlier that year when Alec took over as Professional to run the teaching and the shop. A genial and pleasant character, who had established a friendly tone from the start of the Club, Alf was greatly missed by the members who transferred their goodwill to Alec.

In 1939 it was Tony Englefield's personal pleasure to form a close friendship with Ron Baker when his family moved to Oxted from London at the outbreak of the War. Ron was then helping in the shop as Assistant and, apart from giving TE valuable tips about golf and the course, they spent many happy evenings touring the locals to play darts having some precarious rides on his motorbike, and in search of fun before being called up.

Not content to wait, and full of youthful enthusiasm, they both decided to volunteer for air crew duties in the RAF hoping that they could go through the war together. Such ideas soon faded however, since, although Tony passed the medical requirements for the Pilots Training scheme, Ron had some slight problem and had to be content with the prospect of Navigation/Air Gunner. So they separated for initial training, and to Tony's great shock and sorrow he heard about 12 months later that Ron had suddenly died, having somehow suffocated during his sleep at his RAF quarters. He was only 21. Apart from the tragic and untimely premature death, the natural talent as a virtual scratch golfer, who could play almost equally well left or right handed, had been lost.

Alec, who succeeded his father as pro and remained for 30 more years, had the slow fluid, full elegant swing of a class golfer and probably would have made the top echelon of the UK golfing world if he had not had to enter the Army (1940/45) and spent his best years mostly overseas. The vital time for a golf professional between 20 and 30 had slipped from Alec's career, which had been interrupted just at the prime point where he might have reached heights, even possibly up to the Ryder Cup level. In 1938 he had just missed out to

Ken Bousfield, and he was a strong contender to be selected in 1939. Allegedly Alec was so disappointed at not being able to play in the Ryder Cup because of the war that he rushed off to volunteer at the first opportunity - much to his father's annoyance!

He then served six years in the Army. He saw considerable action in France, Egypt (8th Army), Sicily and Italy where his courage and initiative brought about the capture of an important position for which he was subsequently decorated with the Military Medal and mentioned in dispatches.

So, his familiar tall figure and long sweeping drives became a feature over the years. Many hopeful golfers will have benefited from his guidance, even if they made only modest progress within the limits of their abilities. His patience in encouraging all levels of golfers must often have been tried to the limit, but he seldom showed any signs and was always a most even-tempered teacher.

Alec has the amazing record of having scored, at various times, a 1 or a 2 at every hole on the course (except the 12th).

Alan Waters was Assistant Professional for many years with Alec Baker, from June 1929 to 1941. He got a full Professional's job at Stand, near Manchester, and after a short time he moved to Worplesdon where he remained until he retired. Incidentally he married Betty Goad meeting her when she worked in the kitchen at Tandridge. While at Stand, Alan achieved a high finish in the British Open Championship, actually being in contention at one time.

Amongst many good scores, Alan Water's 64 gross was for several years a record for the course, but this was equalled by Alec in 1951, by Bill Hotton in 1951, and by Ian MacDonald in May 1960.

Leslie Hooker, who was Assistant Pro for several years, and could probably have been a top player if he had not decided to opt out, also did rounds of 65 more than once.

Other Assistants have been Bill Hotton (who moved over to become Club Steward for some years after being involved in a car crash), Jack Ramsden, Ian MacDonald, Howard Francis, John Hamilton, Pat Coombes, Douglas Machray, and other young men. All these have done reasonably well in the golfing world but have not hit the top headlines.

Alec's inherent courteous and modest manner continued the tradition of his family to the Club's advantage and it was entirely fitting that after 50 years at Tandridge on his retirement in 1979 he was made an honorary life member, so that the members could continue to enjoy his company on the course and in the bar. At the presentation of a handsome cheque to him, he regaled the members with many memories of his life at Tandridge (see Appendix 2).

(From l. to r.) Graham Johnston, Mrs Baker, Alec Baker and Kenneth Robinson

Alec's successor was his assistant Allan Farquhar from Scotland, a man with the natural talent one expects from that area. He had a modest manner, but was much liked by members. He served a total of 29 years as Assistant and as Professional until the early months of 1998, when the Committee suggested to him that he should resign due to his ill health. He left at the end of September of that year.

Stephen Farquhar was Assistant to his father for some years, and did much to encourage golf by the Juniors. He left to join Cherry Woods GC in mid-1998.

Chris Evans, a young Professional from Princes GC, was appointed to succeed Allan, and took up his duties on 1st November 1998. He has revitalised the shop and, in the short time he has been with the Club, has already established a reputation as being a skilled teacher. Within a few days of joining the Club, he went round the course in only 66 shots. His young assistant David Evans, who came with him from Princes, is a qualified PGA member and also an accomplished golfer. They have recently been joined by another young professional, Michael Gibson.

Staff

In the early days, Caddie Masters were usual adjuncts to a Golf Course, and still continue in a few places, but, like experienced caddies, this breed seems to be dying out. Sergeant Millen was the first Caddie Master and he had as many as 50 caddies to organise. These he divided into first and second class categories - the initial pay for the first being 2/3d per round, and 1/9d for the second.

Many characters appeared at Tandridge as caddies and their knowledge of the local undulations, best lines, the borrows for putts on all greens, and about the game itself was remarkable. The last regular caddy "Glosby" was a small wizened man who seemed ageless and who easily carried, without demur, any heavy golf bag. A tired and dog-eared cigarette, hand rolled, usually dangled from the corner of his mouth.

The wealth of cryptic and amusing remarks which must have passed between many players and caddies have regrettably disappeared. What a waste of humorous material.

Colonel Bradney (one of the ground staff) suffered from the effects of gas in the First World War, and could only appear at the Club when his lungs allowed. He was a very tall man (about 6ft 6ins) and always marched from bunker to bunker with his rake at the slope in what can only be described as "a smart and soldier-like manner". This was said to be some form of therapy and provided an open air occupation for him. In spite of the high rank he had held in the Army, at Tandridge he was just one of the grounds staff and would always touch his cap and say "Good morning, Sir" when one passed him.

The roll of Head Greenkeepers started with MacDonald, followed by Bill Allen, Higginbotham, Bert Fordham, and now John Bishop (who has been over 40 years on the staff).

The importance of the various Stewards, who, with their wives, so ably handled the catering, bar needs and foibles of members over the years, needs no emphasis.

Starting with the renowned Mrs Brown (a Stewardess with a dominant character who had to be approached on an "off day" with

Bert Fordham "swishing" the 9th green

some caution), the Tandridge reputation for best quality English food began to be established, and for years now this factor has been a well-known feature of the Club.

About 1929 there was one eccentric Stewardess, who had strong opinions against fox hunting. She would leave everything (even if in the middle of a meal) as soon as she saw a hunt in progress and would rush out to try and drag riders off their horses, berating them for taking part in such a cruel sport.

Mrs Collins took over from Mrs Brown. She will be remembered particularly for the doughnuts she used to serve at teatime. She was followed by the Baxters, and then by Bill and Phil Hotton, he having moved indoors from being Alec Baker's assistant following a nasty car accident.

John and Pat Harrison came next, who set a very high standard for many years. John had a nice sense of humour and at the end of one Committee match versus the staff he began his vote of thanks by saying "On behalf of all of us who work here - <u>and</u> the Secretary - ....." They were followed by Peter and Pat Gunner, another cheerful couple.

Paul and Maureen Pigott, who had been assistants to the Harrisons, were invited to return to the Club as Head Steward and wife respectively, after the Gunners left. They were worthy successors and were ably assisted by Alex and Doreen Shipperley and by Les and Doreen Ella. The present Steward, Rasher Smith, joined during the Piggotts' reign and, with Percy Francis, has become well-known and popular both with members and Societies.

Behind the bar - Percy Francis, Gill Challis-Kyle and "Rasher" Smith

During the period when Adrian Furnival was Secretary, a decision was taken to replace the Pigotts with a Head Chef, because of the increased demands for meals both in the evenings and in the Gallery Bar. After an initial disappointment with the person appointed, the Club engaged William Virley, the present Head Chef. He together with Sarah Snashfold and various other assistants now look after all the Club's catering requirements to an extremely high standard. During the last year William has been promoted to House manager with overall responsibility for catering and bar.

Mention must also be made of the Assistant Secretaries, the first of whom was Mary Morley. She joined Ken Evans in 1975 on a part time basis and worked very happily for some 15 years until a decision was taken when Ian Wheater was Secretary that full time help was needed. At the AGM after her departure, she was made an Honorary Member in recognition of her unique contribution to the Club.

Chris Atkinson, William Virley, Alison Deighton, Sarah Snashfold & Jo Whapham

The Admin. team - Jill King, Bob Neve and Albert Weller

Phillipa Colley became the full time Assistant Secretary and again fitted in very well, until her departure in 1994. Her successor is Bob Neve, a retired Senior Customs Officer who in the few years he has been with the Club has brought many of its records and systems up to date. He is also the past Chairman of the Gresham Club.

The Office staff have been completed by an accountant who has kept the accounts for the Club over the years. The first. appointed in October 1988, was Les Lyons, an enthusiastic and likeable character. He was followed by Jan Hobbins who during her time with the Club prepared the claim for the £125,000 VAT refund. The present accountant Jill King - both charming and efficient - has been with the Club since 1995.

In 1994, the Club ran into possible difficulties with the Inland Revenue over whether corporation tax was payable on the profit which it apparently made on its large annual receipts of visitors' green fees. The Club called in an expert - a Mr Ian White, very voluble and likeable - who managed to convince the Inspector of Taxes that no profit was in fact made - at least for a period of years.

The unexpected VAT refund of some £125,000 in 1995 was a pleasant surprise for the Club. At first the Committee felt that this should be passed back to the members pro rata but on reflection decided instead to retain it, putting the money into a separate fund. Over the next three years, it was spent on major improvements to the Club and the course.

Chapter 8

The War Years 1939 - 1945

The Club continued as best as it could during the War. 36 members promptly departed on active service but retained their membership without payment of subscription. If they played they were required to pay a green fee of two shillings and sixpence or four shillings for a full day.

After the "phoney war period", the apparent peace was dramatically altered by the start of bombing raids in 1940. The proximity of R A F Stations at Biggin Hill and Kenley, where famous fighter squadrons were stationed, meant that they were targets for air attack, and Tandridge was near enough to be involved on many occasions.

From September 1940 until the following June the clubhouse became the headquarters of the local battalion of the Local Defence Volunteers (afterwards known as the Home Guard). This was run by the Secretary (C N M Hamilton) as Adjutant and he had a suitably sandbagged hut installed near the 12th/13th hole to get maximum vision.

Early in 1941 a searchlight detachment was stationed on part of the 14th and 17th fairways and 12 huts were erected, but these caused little interference with play.

At the same time the grazing rights on the course were let to a local farmer for his sheep for £50 per annum initially and at £70 from June 1942. In June 1944 the sheep grazing rent was raised to £80 and remained at that figure until the sheep were removed in June 1946. During that time, barriers had to be erected round the verandah to prevent the sheep from seeking shelter there.

In March 1942 the iron railings on the course were requisitioned for the manufacture of munitions, but the railings marking the boundary of the course were not taken.

At the beginning of 1944 the garages were requisitiioned for use by the Surrey War Agricultural Committee. On 21 July a flying bomb fell in the spinney to the east of the clubhouse causing no casualties but extensive damage to the windows, doors, ceilings and the asphalt roof. The following day three barrage balloons were erected near the 3rd, 5th and 10th tees, and at the end of September the searchlight sites were relinquished by the War Office.

Canadian Army officers and men were billeted at The Pheasantry. Tandridge Hall, originally owned by Erroll Holmes (the Surrey and England cricketer) was regrettably burned down owing to wild horseplay by some Canadians billeted there. Sir David Burnett, the present owner, restored part of the Hall as far as possible.

The Commanding Officer at RAF Biggin Hill arranged to be collected by light airplane at Tandridge, landing on the first fairway in case he was needed during a round of golf.

During the War, a bomb made a great crater in the middle of the 12th fairway, just at the point where long hitters aim to play their second shots up to the green. Glanvill Benn remembers that some members were in favour of retaining it as a permanent bunker, but they must have been outvoted.

Despite rations and staff shortages, lunches continued daily under the able hand of Mrs Brown, followed later by Mrs Collins.

Alex Cockburn was out practising on the 16th one day in 1944 when he heard aerial gunfire over Oxted. Later he heard his sister had narrowly escaped being hit in the High Street by random machine gun fire from several Focke-Wulf German fighters. These same planes crossed Tandridge over the 16th fairway and Alex flung himself into one of the bunkers near the tall trees as bullets sprayed around him in the grass. He wondered why he was such an important target!

Tony Englefield also recalls playing a morning round with Ron Baker when a "dog-fight" between Spitfires and Messershmitts, supporting the Junkers 88 bombers, took place overhead. Spectacular vapour trails and aerobatics showed the skill and intensity of attack of the famous "Few", and showers of spent shells fell on the course. They had to decide whether to go for cover but, possibly with foolhardy aplomb, continued playing until a German fighter was seen to emit smoke and start ploughing to the earth with the pilot floating down by parachute. He landed near Oxted and was captured. Strange to record this incident now, but at the time it did not seem so much out of the ordinary way of life.

Chapter 9

Characters over the Years

Arthur Cohen (His Honour Judge) until his death in 1995 had been a member of the Club since it started. His lawyer father is entitled to enormous credit with his colleagues for the founding of the constitution and general organising of the Club. Arthur was a young man in his twenties at the beginning of Tandridge and soon showed his golfing ability by being pulled from handicap 6 to 4 - and subsequently down to scratch. An indestructible, witty, and shrewd character, he contributed much to the Club.

Arthur Cohen

He recalled that many years ago David Blair applied for membership and, being a Scottish international and a Director of Distillers Co Ltd, he hoped for early admission. Not so. The then Secretary (Mr Hamilton - the second) said there was a waiting period of four years or so, despite Mr Blair's low handicap of +2. The result was that Blair gave up his application and joined another Club - to Tandridge's loss. Within a few years he became a member of the Walker Cup team in 1955 and 1961, and won the Scottish Amateur Championship in 1953.

Arthur also remembered that the first Secretary (A.C.Hamilton) had also been a +2 handicap golfer playing for the Oxford and Cambridge Society. He recalled that the hut near the 13th tee used to be available for drinks on Saturdays and Sundays (now ceased).

He was one of four golfers with Alec Baker, Philip Scrutton and Ken Gordon, playing the 7th hole one Sunday when three of them drove the green, and Arthur was just 10 yards off. The three on the green all putted out for 2's and Arthur had a 3 - a total of 9 shots between them.

Memories of a formidable member, **Admiral Ford**, include visions of his peppery countenance and formidable presence. Having been "C in C Malta" during the First World War, he did expect to be constantly in command! A good golfer, whose handicap only went up to 6 when he reached 80 years, he would never allow any further increase despite his declining years and ability. He also took as "given" any putt around 6 feet. Apparently the Admiral was on the 14th fairway one day when Bert Morris was driving a truck which he stopped to let the Admiral play. The Admiral topped the ball about 15 yards and shouted out " Could you do better than that?" Bert was grinning so the Admiral turned to him and put a ball down saying "You think you could do it?". Bert took the Admiral's club and hit the ball about 150 yards straight on to the green - no comments were made by either party!

Another Admiral, **Sir William Goodenough**, also a keen golfer, was a member at the same time. He had been in command at the Royal Naval Dockyard, Chatham and often used to arrive with a coxswain as his caddy. He had a stentorian voice and his bellow across the fairways was a thing of awe. The famous story of his meeting with Bill Maffett took place around the second green when Bill, playing on his own, had pitched his ball on the green and a large figure shouted at him from a distance "Do you want a game? I'm Goodenough". To which Bill replied "OK, but I don't know if I am".

Admiral Goodenough was a hero of the Battle of Jutland (1916) and President of the Royal Geographical Society. He was basically kind and a great friend of the Club, but he adopted the pose of a taciturn sailor of few, but blunt words, and earned a slightly unfortunate reputation. During a slow round Dr Laing was rather impatient to get on so he decided to send a note forward with a caddy to the four ahead asking if he could come through as he had to attend a patient. Admiral Goodenough, who was ahead, returned the note with a cryptic reply "Certainly not".

A prominent politician, standing at the bar one morning, complained of the state of the course and lack of service (the staff did not like him), and the Admiral, reading his paper, looked up and, knowing quite well who the grumbler was, said in a quiet tone, but which could be heard round the room, "I don't know who you are, Sir, but personally I enjoy my membership of this Club. Good morning to you, Sir!"

On another occasion a recently joined American, who had come to live in England to represent a Chicago firm of printing machinery manufacturers, walked into the lounge, slapped the Admiral on the back saying with hearty cheerfulness - "Hiya, Admiral, how yer keeping?" "Barge" Goodenough did not bat an eyelid or say a word until the American, **Martin Slattery**, had moved well away but not out of earshot. Then, in the same quiet but penetrating voice he said, "Who does that damn Yankee think I am - a bloody tin of sardines?"

Subsequently these two contrasting characters became close friends. The Admiral must have played a considerable part in getting Mr Slattery elected to the Committee and, in 1936, Captain. Tandridge thus set an example to the Royal and Ancient, whose first American born Captain, Francis Ouimet, was not elected until 1951.

Martin Slattery was the most generous person and totally devoted to the Club and Captains. The Secretary at the time, the second Hamilton, had the greatest difficulty in restraining him from showering the Club with gifts and prizes which no other future Captain could hope to match. Enough to record that in those lavish pre-war days the winner of the main event that bears his name (the Slattery Trophy) used to receive the splendid trophy to hold for one year plus three new wooden clubs with steel shafts, which were just coming into use, and a gold medal!

Another character was **Sir Ernest Clarke**, a very straight-laced eminent civil servant who became one of the early Captains. Such was the social scene in those days (1920's) that after the Artisans Match with the Club, he spoke in the vein of ...... " we know you men are not of our class, but we do not object to playing you, confident that you will behave yourselves and not bring disgrace on the Club to which you are privileged to be attached........". Such condescending, class-ridden remarks now seem incredible. The Artisans lead by Mr Waters (father of Alan Waters) responded generously and presumably tolerated the situation as it then was.

Another good friend of Tandridge who spent many happy hours on the course and in the Clubhouse was **Tommy Vandervelde**. The beautiful shower of daffodils on the banks behind the 14th green were given by him and provide a most attractive background and reminder every spring. Only two days before he died in July 1981 he wrote to Eileeen and (the late) Ken Evans, then Secretary ...... "I have reached the age of 85 with hardly a day's illness. A splendid life with a happy marriage .... My happiest days have been, (a) my membership at Tandridge with all the friendship I have enjoyed and (b) my fly-fishing in water ..... I wish you and all the members of Tandridge all the best".

Roy Siemssen played a prominent part as Captain (1956) and Trustee of the Club for a long innings. His facetious, or apparently simple queries, at meetings or generally, disguised a shrewd penetrat-

-ion of the real position in a given situation, and his pretended waffling was often a cover - used, as in his expert bridge play, to confuse or to achieve a realistic result.

Roy had the reputation - perhaps unfairly - of often saying when he arrived on the 1st tee "Gosh, I've got a hangover this morning". He would then play his usual skilful game for the rest of the round.....

Roy Siemssen

Amongst some of his more memorable efforts, prior to a lunch when over sixty members were present in the lounge awaiting their turn to be shown to their tables eight at a time, the steward, John Harrison, called for quiet and announced that grace would be said prior to the meal en masse. No sooner had he stopped speaking than up stood Roy and with an air of authority said "Benedictus, benedicat per Christum Dominum nostrum". The room disintegrated in mirth since the senior church member present (Canon Ken Hoare) had been pre-empted before he had time to speak However, after the meal, with all seated in the dining room, the Canon called for silence and gave an "official" grace.

Another of Roy's famous moments occurred on the 3rd green. Tony Englefield recalls: "It was a very cold winter day in 1982, with a touch of white frost on fairways and greens. Gloves were desirable, but Roy carried an elderly handwarmer, a dilapidated item which had seen better days. On arrival at the 3rd green our golf balls were in various places on the putting surface and I was about to putt, when Roy suddenly jumped up and down by the flag, vigorously rubbing his thigh, and shouted "I've been stung by a wasp!" There then emerged a slight puff of smoke from the trouser pocket and soon the offending object was pulled out and hastily flung to the ground."

Roy was also made an Honorary Member of the Club shortly before he died in 1995.

One of the stalwarts and original members of the Club - **George Hankey** (an internationally renowned dental surgeon) - was made a member by his father in 1925. The original Bond holders had the opportunity to bring in family members. George, playing off 14 at that early date, was a steady and determined golfer, and also a member of Royal Ashdown and Ford Manor.

He pointed out that the two prominent noses on the heads carved in wood at the foot of the stairs leading from the lounge to the gallery are alleged to have been inspired by Sir Benjamin Cohen and Admiral Goodenough. There are no records to prove this, or whether this interpretation came after the event.

George recalled the first Summer Dance (1925/6) in a marquee erected on the putting green; that the projected Channel Tunnel (1926) would, if the intended route had been followed, have turned up somewhere around the 12th tee area; and that Roy Siemssen, from the back tee at the 13th shied his first drive out in to the woods, decided the ball was lost without looking for it, and holed his second shot.

He also told of a famous Club match when two well-known members played a combined 25 strokes at the 12th hole, with the winner (at 12) trying to keep the facts subdued.

Glanvill Benn, now living at Aldeburgh, recalls the famous Admiral Goodenough and also F Laming Evans, and certain altercations in the lounge which now, happily, are mercifully forgotten in the mists of time. Glanvill is now the only surviving, original member, having as a schoolboy tied for the first Club medal prize awarded. He was made an Honorary Member of the Club in 1988.

An early picture of Glanvill Benn, with the old clubhouse in the background

Graham Sankey remembered another incident. "During the foursomes at the Autumn Meeting in 1972, Kenneth Robinson and I went forward at the 2nd hole to spot the drives. George drove and the ball was coming straight for me so I moved aside but the ball was hooked and followed me, and hit me on the mouth first bounce breaking my two front teeth which did not matter as they were of George's own manufacture. When he arrived he had to be dissuaded from searching for the bits in the longish grass. George later replaced my teeth free of charge. While he was out of his surgery for a moment his nurse said that she intended to take up golf, so I warned her 'Don't play with him, he knocks your teeth out'".

Graham Sankey

The original 7th tee used to be placed just behind the 6th green (it is still there and sometimes used to save time). Mr Sankey (Senior) and his son Graham were playing a 4-ball with George and his father, and were standing on that old 7th tee. A ball, hit from the 4th tee, came flying over and struck Graham on the head. He dropped as if poleaxed. His father was so infuriated that he rushed down the 4th to strike the erring golfer with an iron, but owing to advanced years he luckily ran out of breath before arriving at his target. Graham recovered and no harm seems to have been done.

Kenneth Robinson is the only man who has been honoured with the Captaincy twice, in 1949 and the Jubilee year 1974. He was President from 1976 to 1981 when he died at the comparatively early age of 68. He acted as Secretary during the illness of Godfrey Brewer and the arrival of Ken Evans. His contribution to the Club's affairs as Committee Member, Captain, Trustee, and President was immense. He gave similar service to the Old Marlburian Golfing Society, and founded the match between that Society and the Club, which is so much enjoyed by both sides.

Geoffrey Heyworth, later Baron Heyworth of Oxton, was also a very distinguished member of Tandridge. There is a book about his career which was produced a few years ago by his firm Unilever, of which he was Chairman.

Another was the **Hon Patrick Bowes Lyon**, the uncle of the Queen Mother. Graham Sankey played with him many times between the wars. He won the Men's Doubles at Wimbledon in 1887, and the following year lost the final to the Renshaw Brothers after being 2 sets all and 5 games all.

Bryan Valentine responded to a suggested lunch date in September 1982, and a hilarious time was spent with this grand extrovert personality. His death in 1983 removed from the cricket world one of the great players, but he also excelled at tennis (where he was at top level, playing "Bunny" Austin and winning), at hockey, squash, snooker and soccer. Any game with a ball came easily to him.

As a golfer he quickly reduced his handicap in his late teens from 18 to 12, and then to 8 and down to 3, before reaching scratch, all within 3 years! His courage and physique were best displayed in the test matches against Australia, and he remembered most clearly the "bodyline" incidents, the fierce Australian fast bowlers and the hostile crowds. His perpetual good humour, stentorian laugh, and strong build were known throughout his native Kent. He gained a blue at soccer and cricket, and won the Public Schools Lawn Tennis Doubles.

In 1933-34 as a leading amateur batsman he made 136 at Bombay for D R Jardine's MCC team in India. He shared in the captaincy of Kent and toured South Africa in the Tests 1938-9 with W R Hammond. This tour included a "timeless" Test match intended to be played to a finish. After 10 days, the boat they had to catch could not wait, so they settled for a draw - 42 runs short - with a score of 654 for 5.

His batting average was 64 for the seven Tests in which he played for England. He was badly wounded in the War, won the M.C., and still took on the captaincy of Kent CC from 1946 to 1948. A man with no enemies.

During a frosty winter day he had driven the 5th green (corroborated) but "I was so excited that I then took 4 putts and lost the hole". A memorable round of his included the first 9 holes in 46, the second 9 in 31, including a hole-in-one at the 13th, a 3 at the 14th, and a 2 at the 15th.

Bryan's father was one of the first Captains at Tandridge (1933). He was one of the best oboeists in the UK and joint partner with DeRougemont in a leading Lloyd's underwriting firm.

Other leading personalities who have been members include **Lord McFadzean**, who had been a Director of Midland Bank, BICC, English Electric, Canada Life Assurance and so on. He was President of the FBI 1959-61, and held the unique title of "Knight of the Thistle", an honour conferred on only 16 people and equivalent to the order of "Knight of the Garter". His award was made as the highest order in chivalry to mark his enormous contribution to the country in export work.

Ken Gordon, their son-in-law, was a scratch golfer at Tandridge (1945-7) before going to America. He also played for Uppingham School in the Halford-Hewitt Cup team with Roy Siemssen. He used to play often with Philip Scrutton and Alec Baker in the top flights of golf.

From 1974 he was the Secretary of the U.S. Professional Golf Association - an important post - Chairman of the U.S. Museum Committee for Golf, and founder of the Moon Club (devised after Alan Shepherd's famous golf shot on the Moon with a telescopic No. 6 iron).

As Secretary of the U.S.G.A., Ken had Arnold Palmer as his Chairman and an eminent Committee of 15, including leading U.S. professional golfers' name and also ex-President Ford.

Alec Baker, playing with **Kenneth Konstam**, a fiery and quick-tempered person (and an international bridge player), had sold him a new set of wooden clubs. Konstam's first shot with the driver went into the trees on the right of the first fairway, so Konstam broke the club over his knee and threw it into the nearest bushes. Alec let the situation cool down and the game proceeded, but when it was over he went to retrieve the broken club and found the brand new (once hit!) club head. He attached a new shaft and made the club complete again.

A week later, Alec handed the restored club to Konstam on the 1st tee and said, "Here is your club, fully repaired". Konstam thanked him and, trying to drive, again scuffed and topped his ball badly into the bushes on the right. In irritation he threw his club after the ball and it landed up in a tree. This time, Alec waited until after the round to recover the club and, after a few minor polishes, he reckoned the owner had no further use for it and eventually sold it to another member.

Fondly known as Terminal (or Cardiac) Alley, the 17th and 18th holes have unhappily claimed some members as victims. **Sam Herbertson** expired near the bunker between the 10th and 18th fairways, having just pulled his not inconsiderable weight up the slope from the 18th tee. **Francis Gill**, a well-known golfer playing off scratch in 1927, died on the front steps of the Clubhouse when visiting it in 1979. **Claude Coulson** (senior) died on the 3rd fairway in 1977 and **Donald Light** (an international hockey player and administrator) died in a chair in the lounge in 1972.

A personal note from a former member - **Maurice Allom** - confirms that as a cricketer he played for Cambridge (1927 and 1928), for Surrey Cricket Club (1927 to 1933), was President of the MCC 1969/70, and President of Surrey for eight years from 1970. His golfing prowess at Tandridge included some lengthy hits, amongst which was a drive on to the 6th green from the back tee - but evidently in frozen conditions which allowed the ball to fly and run. The ball ended on the top edge of the green, but four more shots were needed to slot it. Some other members say that they fondly recall his very pretty young daughter, but they cannot remember what he looked like....

From about 1960 onwards, a fourball, known as "The Olympic Four", often played at 10 a.m., having allowed the early starters to get ahead. This four consisted of the late **Lester Horne, Claude Coulson, Kenneth Cramp and John Corbett.** They had jointly subscribed to Olympic Games Funds, and also presented one of the tables in the Men's Bar to remember many happy years and times spent there.

Sir (Walter) Raymond Birchall, KCB, KBE was Assistant Secretary at the General Post Office in 1934, and later became Director General 1946/49. His title reflected the appreciation for his skill and services during a difficult period just after the war. His handicap was 6 and he passed on some of his knowledge and skill to his son **Vernon**, a steady golfer but, regrettably, now retired to the West Country.

Peter Burles made a significant contribution to the Club after he joined it with his wife Peggy in 1966. He came with a reputation as being a fine, consistent golfer, having won the Boys' Amateur Championship in 1934 by the then record margin of 12 & 10, and the Czech Open Championship in 1938. He became Captain in 1977, was elected President in 1987, a position he held until his untimely death in April 1993. He also played for Aldenham School in the annual Halford Hewitt tournament for some 50 years, and was strongly connected with Aberdovey GC where he was elected its Captain in its Centenary Year 1992.

Peter Burles

A friendly fourball (from l. to r.) George Tweeddale, Bill Stow, Graham Johnston and George Aitkenhead

Many other golfers also are worth remembering, such as **Bill Hunter** and **Jack Rendell** who spent many happy years at the Club, the latter serving as Hon Treasurer for many years. Another prevented from being elected Captain because of his fatal illness was **Tim Gourlay**, best known for his short shorts and long but occasionally wild tee shots. He was christened Mr Heineken because his ball often reached parts that no other players could reach.

Then there were the well known partnerships that used to play together in Club competitions or on a Sunday morning - **Stewart** & **Bangert, Waylett** & **Giggins, Drury** & **Siemssen**, **Stow** & **Johnston,** and **Coulson** & **Forbes-Watson** to name just a few.

Interesting Scores

An old Tandridge record dated 6 April 1929 shows that a fourball consisting of **Arthur Cohen, G Gough, F Sutherland Gill and G Jenner** had a best ball of 65, which included both teams playing the 18th, 1st and 2nd holes in 3 strokes each.

Arthur Giggins once played the four short holes in 7 shots - i.e. 2, 2, 2 and 1 (15th). **Catherine Bailey** and **Bob Howie** have done all four short holes in 1.

Bob Taylor played all the short holes in 2 each, as did **Cecil Harrison** when over 80 years of age. The latter also went round in only 78 shots when aged 81.

Graham Sankey was playing with Edgar Wren in the Captain's Prize on 25 September 1965. Edgar's drive at the 7th did not reach the fairway and Graham holed the next for a 2. He then holed in 1 at the 8th with the same club. They got 8 points for those two holes and a total of 16 for the whole round. In those days the Captain's Prize was a Stableford Foursome with partners drawn; it was altered to its present form in 1976 by Richard Rawlings.

An air shot by **Jack Hamer** on the 1st tee was followed by a near-miss, which just trickled the ball down the steps to hit Graham Johnston's golf bag. This in accordance with the rules at once disqualified Graham from the hole, and despite Jack's protestations to overlook it, Graham adhered strictly to the loss of the hole.

The first Secretary (**A C Hamilton**) playing with a Mr Hood had a hole-in-one at the 4th. To celebrate this Mr Hood sent a dozen red rose bushes to be planted at The Pheasantry - possibly some still survive.

The same Secretary had a cat called "Sam" who used to sit on the gate at the Pheasantry and watch the world go by. Rumour has it that a fourball was on the 11th tee with a ball ready teed up when Sam darted over and knocked the ball off the peg. It is thought that no penalty was incurred. On another day, a ball was putted up to 3 inches from the hole on the 10th green when Sam reportedly suddenly skipped forward and pawed the ball into the hole. Allegedly, Arthur Cohen, whose ball it was, exclaimed: "Oh good, rub of the green - down for 3!"

Roy Siemmsen, when playing his first round at Tandridge in order to get a handicap, started with a 9 and then did the rest of the holes in level par. The Secretary awarded him a handicap of 2.......

Roger Whitmore once did the last five holes in level threes compared with the par of 4,3,4,4 & 4. Playing in a fourball with Jim Butcher, Kevin Wylie and John Wilson, they all got 3s at the 7th (Kevin Wylie driving the green), and completed the 18 holes in two hours.

John Berry once had six threes in a row - from the 3rd until the 8th inclusive. **Duncan Ferguson** repeated this feat, from the 11th to 16th, at which stage his partner (a visitor) decided he had had enough and went in !

Brian McConnell got a four at his first hole the 10th hole, a three at the 11th, and a two at the 12th. History does not record what he scored at the 13th but it was not a 1.

John and Jean Wilson playing in a foursomes stableford with the Howies scored 16 points in four holes with gross birdies at the 6th, 7th, 8th and 9th - but only scored 25 points over the remaining 14 holes.

Whilst playing the 16th hole in a friendly fourball in 1997 with John McKirdy, Tony Skivington and Brian Teakle, **Peter Heilbron** put his second shot 6 inches from the hole. The other three were also on the green in two shots. After Peter had holed out, Tony followed in from 6 ft, and Brian from 9 ft. John said "You're are making it very difficult for me" being 15 feet away - but then also holed his putt, making four gross birdies.

Chapter 10

The Ladies

Elizabeth Yule - Lady Captain 1998/99

The first meeting of Tandridge lady members is shown as taking place at Lloyds Bank, Oxted on 26 September 1924. **Mrs Forwood, Mrs Leach** plus **Miss Anne Stewart** (first Secretary) and A C Hamilton (in attendance) decided on basic items, including the election of 33 members, a ladies' monthly medal for a gold safety pin, and prospective prizes and cups.

Jean Hamilton (A C Hamilton's daughter) had been a pupil teacher in 1927 at The Hill House, Westerham. Oliver Roberts recalls being one of the pupils at The Pilgrims where A C Hamilton was Headmaster, and memories still linger of some painful occasions following inattention, when the famous line "this hurts me more than you" was used.

Jean had started golf at Limpsfield Chart at about the age of 10. In a match against Banstead, she was noticed and her potential was referred to by a lady opponent. This proved to be rather accurate.

In 1928, she won a long driving contest at Tandridge, her drives averaging over 200 yards. From 1930 she played for ten years in the Surrey Ladies County team. She was Captain in 1934, Surrey Champion in 1937, and represented Surrey in the English County Finals (winning several times). She was selected and played in 1937, '38 and '39 for England against Scotland, Ireland and Wales. Her handicap had by then become scratch. In the Home Internationals at Turnberry in 1937, she (and England) won all their matches.

She was a beaten finalist in the Worplesdon Mixed Foursomes in 1935, playing with S Forsyth. Jean also recorded an unofficial score of gross 68 in 1937 at Tandridge.

She was elected Captain of the Club in 1932, 1940, 1964 and in the Jubilee year 1974. She was made an Honorary Member of Surrey in June 1994. Her well known smooth, easy swing continued to grace the Club's course until her death in 1998.

Wonderful scrap books exist, full of great interest and achievements. She was many times reported in the national papers. In 1947 she played international golf in South Africa, and entered the Zululand and Natal Championships becoming Champion of both.

Another eminent personality was **Jo Hicks** OBE, a member who rose to be Captain of the County (Surrey Ladies County Golf Association) in 1950, then President in 1965. In 1963 she became Chairman of the English Ladies' Golf Assocation, President from 1975-77 and a Vice President until her death.

Jean Hamilton *"personifies perfect equilibrium and controlled balance"*
Quoted in *Master Golfers in Action*

In 1971 she was appointed Chairman of the Executive Council of the Ladies Golf Union for two years. She was also non-playing Captain of the English team in the 1952 Home Internationals. She was supported by **Catharine Benn** MBE who also brought honour to Tandridge as President of Surrey (1974-76) and is now a Vice-President. In 1976 she was appointed Chairman of the Executive Committee of ELGA.

Pat Bissett was elected Captain of Surrey in 1971 and 1972, after having been County Competition Secretary for some four years.

Alice Monk was elected Captain of the County for 1975 and 1976 and elected President for 1983, 84 and 85. Mrs Hicks, Mrs Benn and Mrs Monk all received the honour of Honorary Membership of the County.

Another member, **Sue Birley** was Surrey Girl Champion in 1959 and Surrey Champion in 1972. She represented Surrey in the 70s, 80s and 90s, was elected Captain of the County for 1983 and 1984, and became its President in 1996 and 1997. Sue with **Catherine Bailey** represented the County in the English County finals. Tandridge must be very proud of having two of their Lady members in the team of 8, bearing in mind there are over 60 Clubs in the county.

Sue Birley and Catherine Bailey

A word about Catherine Bailey. On 3rd August 1982 she completed a round in 68 gross, on the next day recorded 72 gross, her handicap being reduced from 1 to scratch, then to plus 1 in two days - an outstanding achievement by a dedicated golfer. She won the British Senior Ladies Championship in 1988 & 1989, and was runner up in 1986, 1991 and 1992. She was the English Ladies Senior Champion on four occasions and was runner up in three other years. She was Surrey Ladies champion in 1988 and runner up twice.

Catherine also played in the English Senior Ladies 1st team no less than seven times, captaining it in three of them. As a founder Committee member of ESLGA she represented them in the inaugural European Seniors Individual Championship in the Hague in 1996 and again in 1998 in Switzerland. She represented Surrey in the 1st and 2nd teams in the 70's, 80's and 90's. She also holds the Ladies course record at Tandridge - 67 on 8th August 1995.

Various Ladies' trophies are regularly contested by the Tandridge Ladies. The Hicks Trophy, a 5 a side scratch team event (originally a competition run by The Star newspaper) is a knock-out played between Surrey Clubs. Tandridge won in 1978 and 1988, and were runners up in 1979, 1981, 1987 and 1990.

The Druce Trophy is another Surrey Trophy - a one day eclectic competition, in which a silver and bronze pair play an 18 hole medal round in the morning and another silver and bronze pair try in the afternoon to better the morning score. One quarter of the combined players handicaps are deducted from the eclectic score to produce the winners. Tandridge won in 1973, 1979, and 1994, and were runners up in 1978 and 1985.

The Pearson Trophy for ladies with handicaps between 13 and 34 is played for by the four Home Counties, Surrey, Kent, Essex and Middlesex. Surrey clubs play home and away matches (team of 7) to produce a final Club team who go forward to a semi-final and final with the other three Counties. Tandridge won in 1973.

The London Foursomes is an Inter-Club scratch knock-out foursomes tournament, open to Clubs within 45 mile radius of London, each Club entering 1 pair. Tandridge won in 1980 and 1983, both times with Sue Birley and Catherine Bailey. They together also won the Surrey scratch foursomes Club knock-out no less than seven times - in 1980, 1983, 1985, 1989, 1991, 1992 and 1993. They were runners up in 1981.

THE PEARSON TROPHY 1973

Back row : Sheila Neal-Rand, Joan Freeman, Vida Ness, Joan Plews, Catherine Bailey, Fiona McConnell
Front row : Eve Forbes-Watson, Ruth Harrison, Gladys Harper.

THE HICKS TROPHY 1978

Jean Hamilton, Peggy Burles, Sue Phillips, Janet Sellman, Eileen Howie and Catherine Bailey (Team Captain)

Jean Knight and **Joan Kemp** won the Surrey foursomes in 1950.

Jean Wilson (nee Knight) and Joan Birchall (nee Kemp)

Many lady members of Tandridge enter and enjoy open meetings at other Clubs. Those members who are individual members of the County play in many of the meetings organised for all categories of handicaps by the County.

Lady playing members are limited to 126, and numerous mixed competitions are enjoyed throughout the season. At one time, Gordon & Mary Morley were the only pair to win the Club's Mixed Foursomes in successive years, but this record has been equalled in the past two years by Anne Hughes playing with her son David.

Exhibition matches with ladies at Tandridge have included firstly the 1962 match, when Angela Bonallack and her sister-in-law Sally Barber played against Ruth Porter and Bridget Jackson. The ladies at the 1st started with three fours and a three. At the 10th Bridget Jackson hooked her drive well to the left but was on the green in 2 with an enormous shot over the trees. In 1971, Brian Huggett and

Neil Coles took on Angela Bonallack and her sister-in-law Sally Barber, a game which the ladies just won.

In 1984, the Surrey ladies team came to Tandridge to challenge the Men. As a handicap they were asked to play from the men's tees, but this proved to be just too much of a handicap, with the home team winning easily.

In 1994, Catherine Bailey (when Ladies Captain) organised a "Skins Game" comprising Julie Hall (England), Mhairi Mackay (Scotland), Vicki Thomas (Wales) and Clare Hourihane (Ireland). Some wonderful golf was played that day, including incredibly long drives from Mhairi Mackay, and a superb, faded three iron off the tee at the 12th by Julie Hall which enabled her to score a 3 at that hole. The day raised over £7,000 for four charities.

On 26 October 1982, a resolution to appoint a Vice Captain was approved by the necessary 2/3rds of those present at the Ladies AGM. There was a discussion at the end of November 1993 as to whether the Ladies should attempt to obtain voting rights at the Club's AGM, and they achieved this in 1994 when the Club rules were changed. For some years they have had a lady member on both the Golf and House sub-committees.

The Ladies have kindly provided all the flowers in the clubhouse since 1949.

Ladies Club Trophies and Competitions

Ladies Championship - Howie Trophy   36 holes scratch medal.

Burles Trophy   36 holes handicap medal played at the same time as the Ladies Championship. Handicap limit 28.

Lloyd Cup   Summer singles knock-out with handicap limit of 30.

Claxton Teapot   Knock-out open to those beaten in the 1st and 2nd round of the Lloyd Cup.

Rabbits Cup   Knock-out singles for handicaps 28 - 40.

Veterans Cup   18 holes medal for those aged 50 and over.

Evergreens Cup   18 holes medal for those aged 65 and over. Usually played on the same day as the Veterans Cup.

Ross Trophy   Foursomes knock-out played in the Summer. Handicap limit 34.

Benn Foursomes   Fouromes Winter knock-out. Handicap limit 34.
Foster Salver   Winter singles knock-out. Handicap limit 30.

Oliff-Lee Trophies   Club foursomes medal played in conjunction with the qualifying round of the Coronation foursomes.

Coronation Foursomes   Winners go through to area competition.

Captain's Prize   Competition format chosen by the Lady Captain.

Captains' Bowl   Competition open to past and present Captains.

Hospital Cup   Par competition.

Nursing Cup   Medal competition.

Temple Trophy   18 holes stableford in aid of cystic fibrosis.

National Playing Fields Shield   White Elephant stableford competition over 16 holes and with 5 clubs.

Bland Trophy   18 holes stableford for handicaps 28 - 40.

Cancer Relief   combined with July stableford.

Forbes-Watson Trophy   36 holes stableford handicap limit 40.

Summer Foursomes   Bring and Buy, partners drawn.

LGU Pendant   Winner of September medal

LGU Medals   Brooches and certificates presented by the LGU for 4 best nett medal scores Silver and Bronze during the year.

Eclectic Competition   Summer, in aid of the Red Cross.

Plews Trophies   Silver & Bronze winners of Winter eclectic.

Cohen Cup   Best nett score at Spring meeting.

Tanner Bowl   Best nett score at Autumn meeting.

Dunbar Trophy   Silver division aggregate scratch scores Spring and Autumn meetings.

Robinson Cup   Bronze division aggregate scratch scores Spring and Autumn meetings.

Hamilton Cup   Silver division aggregate nett scores Spring and Autumn meeting.

Monk Trophy   Bronze division aggregate nett scores at Spring and Autumn meetings.

Simm Cup   Best 3 nett scores in the year in Silver division.

Webster Trophy   Best 3 nett scores in the year in Bronze division.

Bailey Trophy   Medal round for all prizewinners during the year.

Methuselah Trophy   Open to Ladies and Men over 60.

Chapter 11

The Suggestion Book

The Club still has the same Suggestion Book as it had in 1924. The following extracts give an indication of things that have been troubling members over the years (S = Suggestion, R = *Reply by the Captain up to 1957, thereafter by the Secretary, both on behalf of the Committee*).

A. Course & Golf

1928   S.   That players without caddies be allowed to go through.
         R.   *We disagree with this revolutionary suggestion.*

1928   S.   Jenner protested about back tees being too difficult viz 2nd, 5th, 12th, 14th & 16th.
         R.   *Two have been put out of use (14th & 16th).*

1930   S.   Greens are too slow.
         R.   *New machines have been ordered to deal with this problem.*

1931   S.   Lower half of 16th green should be abolished.
         R.   *Being dealt with.*

1933   S.   That gorse between 14th & 17th fairways be thinned.
         R.   *No further cutting of gorse or bunkers - course too easy.........*

1937   S.   Notice on 16th tee to say whether pin on upper or lower half.
         R.   *Agreed.*

1954   S.   That a practice ground be made in the area between the 2nd, 3rd & 7th fairways.
         R.   *Too far from Club to justify.*

1966   S.   H K Claxton complained about "being behind a funereal fourball composed of ghastly players who knew little about golf and less about the etiquette of the game".

	R.	*This unhappily worded suggestion has been considered by the Committee who have decided to take no action.*
1968	S.	Bunker on 10th fairway be moved 50 yards nearer 10th tee.
	R.	*Has been considered on many occasions since 1924 but opinion is, and was, to leave as is.*
1972	S.	Get rid of ridiculous bunker on 10th/18th.
	R.	*No - essential hazard to 10th - can be seen from 18th.*
1973	S.	Trees cut back in front of 2nd tee.
	R.	*Upward growth is OK, but further advice being obtained on whether fairway should be moved more to the left.*
1977	S.	Course in worst condition of any in 20 mile radius. Can something be done e.g. get outside expert advice, temporary labour, more money on dressings etc.
	R.	*STRI being consulted. Things are beginning to improve.*
1980	S.	Many complaints about hardness of bunkers, quality of sand etc.
	R.	*New sort of sand being tried.*
1986	S.	Captain's "poop" at 15th unsafe and should be removed.
	R.	*Strengthened instead.*
1989	S.	Suggest bell on right of 2nd fairway.
	R.	*Under consideration, but not necessary.*
1990	S.	Path alongside 18th green to be grassed over.
	R.	*Committee believe present decision should stand.*
1990	S.	Having been away for 10 years, am horrified at state of course.
	R.	*Caused by drought of '89, failure of watering system and dry Spring of '90.*
1990	S.	Can nothing be done about shallow bunker on 10th/18th.
	R.	*To be discussed at next Committee meeting.*
1991	S.	A plea to restore 17th to its original style, with tee back below 16th green.

	R.	*Hawtree (architect) being consulted.*
1992	S.	Plea that foursomes/fourballs be allowed on Tuesday am.
	R.	*Not thought to be a good idea.*
1992	S.	Willow trees be planted on left of 2nd green.
	R.	*Good idea.........*
1993	S.	Caddy car to be provided for Captain or Secretary.
	R.	*Not agreed.*
1993	S.	Bell on 2nd to be moved to left of fairway.
	R.	*Committee are reviewing.*
1993	S.	Committee should try to uphold the original bunker designs by H S Colt.
	R.	*Yes - reason why Hawtree (golf course architect) was engaged to advise.*
1995	S.	150 yards markers on fairways not visible.
	R.	*Committee want to leave.*
1996	S.	More VAT refund money to be spent on fairways.
	R.	*Improvement paid from general fund.*

B. House and Catering

1928	S.	Dance to be held.
	R.	*Being considered by Committee.*
1928	S.	The Architects's report is unconvincing and a mistake now might cause lasting inconvenience. We can hardly be expected to be lucky enough to have another fire.
	R.	*The Committee regret such an observation in the Suggestion Book.*
1931	S.	That an excellent local ale Westerham XX be supplied on draught.
	R.	*Committee propose to supply this beer but will not substitute it for present brand which is much liked.*
1932	S.	That a box containing water and a brush be provided on some tees.

	R.	*A tap is provided at corner of clubhouse. Considered this should suffice.*
1934	S.	That a weather vane be erected on or near the clubhouse.
	R.	*Committee do not feel justified in spending Club's money on such luxuries.*
1938	S.	That a charge of 3d for a splash of soda is too high.
	R.	*The charge for a whisky and soda is 1/=. No reduction can be made if only a splash is taken.*
1963	S.	That an improvement is needed in the standard of meat carving at lunch.
	R.	*Don't shoot the pianist - he's doing his best......*
1965	S.	Food is excellent, but ruined by bad carving.
	R.	*Regret can do no more.*
1967	S.	A Club tie.
	R.	*Not yet........*
1966 & 1969	S.	Complaint that no tea available after 6 pm.
	R.	*Will be provided up to 6.30 pm.*
1970	S.	A dinner for gentlemen members.
	R.	*Committee agree that a social evening should be organised, but has doubts as to whether this would be the most popular. Committee are making further enquiries........*
1972	S.	Refurbishment of men's bar is overdue.
	R.	*Expenditure on exterior repairs has meant that internal work must wait until next Spring.*
1972	S.	Fruit machine to be changed.
	R.	*Looking at idea of swopping with another Club.*
1976	S.	Notice board opposite 'phone booth to be allocated to juniors.
	R.	*Agreed.*
1992	S.	Allowing ladies into men's bar is a serious threat to the traditions of the Club.
	R.	*Only permitted after 2.30 pm, to meet need for a "spike bar" for afternoon mixed matches.*

1993	S.	Now Gallery Bar is open, can men's bar be brought back to men only.
	R.	*Agreed.*
1994	S.	Satellite TV in Gallery Bar.
	R.	*Agreed.*
1994	S.	Cleaning service for clubs and shoes to be reinstated.
	R.	*Not agreed.*
1996	S.	New showers : floor slippery and some hooks needed.
	R.	*Shower curtains lengthened, and hooks are in vestibule.*
1996	S.	Use of Men's bar to be restricted to members only.
	R.	*Not accepted by Committee.*
1997	S.	Loudspeakers to be provided in lounge, dining room and gallery bar.
	R.	*Being considered and costed.*

C. Caddies

1931	S.	Complaint about the too heavy clothing caddies are now expected to carry. Suggest some limit be set (which might be of help to the 2.5 million unemployed).
	R.	*Regret that not possible to place limit on bag & contents. Would have to be adopted by whole golfing world.*
1935	S.	That the caddy shelter be improved.
	R.	*Brazier and benches already provided. Useless to provide tables as they are soon broken up.*
1938 & 1939	S.	Plea that caddies be reserved for members & guests up to 10 am.
	R.	*Committee regret that this idea unworkable.*

D. Other

1940	S.	That entrance fees be abolished for duration of the war.
	R.	*Committee do not agree.*

1970	S.	Complaint by Graham Sankey (supported by about 40 others) that no need to have a full time Assistant Secretary.
	R.	*In best interests of the Club.*
1992	S.	Any major change to clubhouse should be discussed with members first.
	R.	*Has been done.......always the Committee's intention so to do.*
1997	S.	Any plans for millenium celebrations ?
	R.	*Committee prefer to concentrate on our own, 75th anniversary celebrations in 1999.*
1997	S.	Committee minutes should be posted on noticeboard.
	R.	*No - any important decisions are promulgated already.*
1998	S.	Much talk about big plans for car park. Should be explained to members.
	R.	*Comment noted.*

Chapter 12

The Gresham and Limpsfield Chart Golf Clubs

Many of the original Tandridge Club members had started golf at Limpsfield, and their transfer to the new Club caused no immediate gap as many people retained dual membership. This was probably because Limpsfield had a category called "Family Membership". Father was the member and his wife and children could play from Monday to Friday without green fee.

Alf Baker was recorded as the winner of the Bogey Challenge Cup in 1919 and, as already stated, served as professional for some years before starting at Tandridge with his son to follow. Caddies at Limpsfield Chart received 6d per round in 1920 plus an extra 3d to clean a set of clubs thoroughly, including burnishing the iron blades with emery cloth.

The Gresham Artisans Golf Club was founded way back in 1895, the common land at Limpsfield Common being already earmarked for golf. With its excellent close-knit smooth grass, it provided a natural forum in an attractive semi-wooded area with just enough undulations and varying if shortish length holes.

An "Artisan" was defined as "someone who works with hands", probably deriving from the craftsman whose "art" was his job. This category somehow turned out to produce many very useful golfers, whose available time for what is usually a protracted game must have been limited.

Cedric Heaysman, who was Captain of the Gresham Artisans Club at Limpsfield Chart in 1982, gave personal details of his long association with this group of keen and modest golfers. His familiarity with the Club's Minute Books since 1921 was a useful source of information.

A "Veteran Cup" was presented in 1895 at the origins of the Club by Mr Keeler (the local village tailor) - so it became known as "The Village Cup". Other cups to be played for annually included "The Glosby Cup" (a piece of silver brought from Canada); "The

Tandridge Cup" (presented by the late Kenneth Robinson and played at Tandridge in the late afternoon); and the "Alf Baker putter", played for as a medal round. This old style putter is made with a special brass plate screwed into the contact surface to which annual tabs are attached with each winner's name engraved on it.

The name "Gresham" came from the Leveson-Gower Estate, being part of that family's lineal descendants' names and the "Grasshopper" emblem, shown on the ties and being the name of the local public house, also derives from that family's crest. The Gresham play annually against Tandridge "A" and "B" teams and also against Tandridge Ladies, all being both home and away fixtures.

Neil Simmons was an excellent artisan golfer, scoring 67 (net 64) whilst playing at Tandridge in July 1962. Leslie Hooker, also a fine golfer, might have aspired to the highest professional ranks if he had persevered, but he declined to pursue the path of excellence. Among his many good rounds, he achieved 69 gross (65 net) at Tandridge as recently as July 1982 after little practice.

John Hooker was a President of the Artisans National Association, a recent Captain and, until his death in 1993, Chairman of the Gresham Artisans. He recalled details of the first years at Tandridge, and how Sergeant Millen, the first Caddiemaster, had no less than 40 to 50 caddies at the weekends. These men signed their names on arrival at the Club and were allocated strictly in order of precedence - some of the old-timers, Glosby, Neaves, Claude Williamson, etc would arrive at 7.30 a.m. to ensure one round, or possibly two. A casual caddie could earn about 10 shillings over the whole weekend with fees and tips.

One of the caddies' first tasks was to go to the starter's hut which still stands on the path leading to the first tee and collect a starting time for which a disc was handed out by the starter. Sergeant Millen put the current starting number in a bracket attached to the hut which could be seen from the Men's changing room.

There are about 32 Artisan Clubs in Surrey alone and most belong to the Artisans National Association, founded in 1921. Such a Club never developed at Tandridge, but the link over many years with the "Gresham" has been a very happy connection from the start.

Chapter 13

Tandridge Today

1974 marked the 50th year of the Club's foundation, and various celebrations were arranged. The first match which had ever been played at Tandridge (1925 against the Parliamentary Golfing Society) was revived; a Jubilee's Day of golf was instituted as an annual event; a Summer Ball took place with a marquee installed over the putting green; and a Pro Am with several very well known golfers competing made a most enjoyable day for the Tandridge members who took part.

Golf

The golfing activities at Tandridge are now almost reaching the maximum possible within a Members' Club.

Medals or stablefords are played on one Saturday in most months throughout the year. In addition some cups are awarded on special occasions e.g. the **Duveen** Cup on Easter Saturday, the **Farr** Cup in August, and the **Clarke** Cup v. bogey in October. The **Saunders Memorial Putter** is played for in May, in which the top eight scores qualify for a singles knockout. A **Prize Winners** Competition - open only to winners of singles competitions held during the year - is held in October of each year.

The **Spring** and **Autumn** meetings which attract large entries are now played on one day. Those wishing to play in both the singles and foursomes competitions begin at very early starting times (in threes) in the morning to give them time to enjoy lunch before playing again in the afternoon. Those only wishing to play in the singles competition have late morning starting times, again in 3s, starting from the 1st tee. Until this system was devised by Kenneth MacLean about three years ago, for a short time the entries were divided into two groups - some to play on the Saturday, the remainder on the Sunday. However this proved to be unsatisfactory as in practice few played on the Sunday. Prior to that, both meetings were held on one day only, but the numbers had to be resticted to 90, with normal starting times for both the morning and afternoon competitions. This often meant little time for lunch for those wishing to play in both competitions.

The Men's **Invitation Meeting** held early in June is two rounds of foursomes stableford, with players who start at the odd holes in the morning being required to begin at the even holes in the afternoon (and vice versa). Entries have to be limited to 60 pairs and the event is nearly always oversubscribed. The **Zig Zag** have their own Invitation Meeting held mid week later that month, comprising just one round of foursomes stableford. A **Seniors Invitation Meeting** has been started recently in August in which up to 60 Zig Zaggers invite as their guests members from other Clubs played in Zig Zag matches. The event is another 18 holes foursomes stableford, the only proviso being that everyone taking part must be aged 60 or over on the day.

The **Club Championship** which is a 36 holes scratch medal takes place in early July, alongside the **Armada Plate** (36 holes handicap) and the **Blake Thomas** Trophy (handicap prize for those aged 60 or more, scored in the morning round). The first winner of the Club Championship, when it was begun in 1966 as a knock-out, was J G C Knight.

These three combined events are the start of the Club's **Golf Week**. It includes a novelty evening competition over 9 holes on the Tuesday, Breakfast golf with a shot gun start to a fourball Texas Scramble starting at 5 am on the Friday, and the **Peter Burles Memorial Aberdovey Bowl** played on the Saturday. This is an 18 holes foursomes stableford where the winners are the highest combined score of both pairs from a team of four (of men, ladies or juniors). This format was the one used at Aberdovey GC, when Peter Burles was its Captain in their Centenary year. A Tandridge team consisting of Leslie Bailey with Norman Parker, and Colin Thomas with John Wilson, managed to win - and bring home - the trophy in its Centenary competition against teams from various other Clubs associated with Aberdovey.

The **Coronation Plates** are an 18 holes knockout competition limited to 16 pairs of members and their guests, and played on the Saturday and Sunday of the second May Bank holiday. There are consolation events for those knocked out on both Saturday and Sunday, plus a cocktail party on the Saturday evening for all competitors. Peter and Jean Heilbron have recently given the **Heilbron Spoons** as a trophy for the winners of the consolation stableford on the Sunday afternoon. In the 1950s, there were sufficient entries to have five rounds of match play with the consolation event taking place with the final on the Monday afternoon. The **Benn Trophy** - now a mixed event open to members and guesrts - was given originally for the consolation event also held on the Monday.

A **Novelty Competition** takes place on the Friday of that weekend, in which a special 10 hole course (devised by John Wilson) is played in which competitors receive "bisques" equal to 1/2 of their handicap. This is open to men members and their male guests. Some of the holes played are interesting e.g. from the 10th tee to the 17th green, the 18th tee to the 14th green, the 17th tee to the 10th green, the old 4th tee to 3rd green, and - best of all - from the 4th tee down to the 2nd green. When this competition began in 1962, the course was a different one (see illustration on next page). It was over 11 holes and included one from the 5th tee to the 11th green, but the trees have grown to such an extent over the years and now make that hole impossible. Competitors are invited to take part in a long driving competition after finishing their round that evening.

One of the best holes in the Novelty competition - from 4th tee to 2nd green

SPECIAL BOGEY COMPETITION

Competitor's Name _____

Handicap _____

ENTER GROSS SCORE AND NUMBER OF BISQUES USED AT EACH HOLE

Signed:
Competitor _____
Marker _____

FOR RULES SEE OVER ➡

MARKER'S SCORE		HOLE NO.	FROM TEE	TO GREEN	BOGEY	GROSS SCORE	BISQUES USED	+ OR −
+ OR −	GROSS SCORE							
		1	10	17	4			
		2	18	14	4			
		3	15	16	3			
		4	10	8	5			
		5	6	7	3			
		6	8 VIA 2ND	3	5			
		7	4	5	4			
		8	11	6	3			
		9	5	11	4			
		10	12	13	4			
		11	14	18	5			
		TOTALS			45			

The card for the original Novelty Competion course

Entries for the **Dinner Foursomes,** played on the morning after the Men's Dinner, are resticted to those who attend the dinner.

The **Hospital (Amenities Fund) Challenge** Cup - in which the entry fees are passed to the local hospital - is a fourball better ball competition against par, played on a Sunday morning in June.

The **Methuselah** Trophy is another 18 holes stableford, open only to men aged 65 and over and ladies aged 60 or over, in which the handicap allowance is based on the age of each competitor.

The Captain and past Captains of the Club compete early in September each year for the **Past Captains' Salver.** The competition is preceded by lunch for which the menu is chosen by the current Captain who also pays for the pre-lunch drinks...... At one time, the format was changed so that the golf took place in the morning followed by lunch, but it reverted back to the current timetable after only a few years. The Board showing names of the winners of the Past Captains' Salver was presented jointly by Kenneth Robinson and George Hankey, the salver itself being presented initially incognito (later disclosed as George Dunbar).

The **Captain's Prize** day has always been immensely popular, especially after the format was changed by Richard Rawlings when he was Captain from drawn foursomes to the present one - a better ball score from a team of three, made up of one low, one medium and one high handicap player. The winning score is usually in the mid 50s. Gary Skivington once distinguished himself by recording only 31 shots over the first nine holes. On another occasion, only two of the three contributed to the team's winning score, but the third member did make the thank you speech to the Captain at the prizegiving ! By tradition the Captain kindly provides refreshments at the half way stage.

There is to be a special **Pro Am** competition on Saturday 14th August this year.

For some years now, John Wilson has organised a day out for members and their guests at **Royal Cinque Ports Golf Club, Deal** at the end of April each year. Competitors play six holes of foursomes with each person within their team of four for both morning and afternoon rounds. Any pair which score 13 or more points over their six holes each win a golf ball.

There is also an unofficial match each year against RCPGC over two days, which was started by Graham Sankey and Jack Aisher some time ago, and is now continued by Mike Holman for Tandridge and by Tim Lloyd (Tandridge's former Secretary, now resident in Deal) for RCPGC.

The Club organises several stroke play mixed competitions. As well as a regular **mixed foursomes** event on a Sunday afternoon usually once per month, there is the **Knight** Trophy (played on Easter Monday), the **Jubilee** Trophy (a St Andrew's greensome with drawn partners, played on the first May Bank holiday), the **Benn** Trophy, the **Cohen** Trophy (in June), a new competition the **Monk** Foursomes (in which husbands may not play with their wives), the **Howie** Quaich (played on the Monday of the August Bank holiday, with some handicap restrictions), and the **Forbes Watson** Trophy (drawn pairs, played at the end of September).

One event which - sadly - now only attracts a few entries is the **Novelty** competition on Boxing Day. This is a foursomes stableford where an additional handicap allowance is given according to the number of clubs a player is carrying e.g. 8 clubs and over the allowance is nil whereas playing only two clubs means seven additional strokes. It is open to both members and guests.

In 1998, a **PG Wodehouse Golf Day** was run, which provided much amusement for the several members of the Wodehouse Society UK and Tandridge who took part in it.

Competitors gather at the P G Wodehouse Golf Day

Various knockout competitions are held throughout the year. The most important of these is the **Lloyd** Challenge Cup which is the singles competition for all players, under handicap. Past winners have included R J Hall (5 times) and P J Hughes (4 times). There are also two separate scratch knockouts - the **Slattery** Trophy for players with handicaps of 12 and under, and the **Doubleday** Divot for those with handicaps between 13 and 17.

The **Rabbits** Cup is a singles knockout for those with handicaps of 18 and over. The **Freeman** Cup is a handicap knockout, with entries restricted to players aged 60 and over on the 1st March, and no matches may be played at weekends or on Bank holidays.

The **Bernard Robinson** is a similar event, open to both full and 5 day members, and entrants must be aged 65 or more on 1st April.

The **Hankey** Bowl is a foursomes knockout, and the **Limpsfield Sick Fund** Challenge Cup is one for fourballs. In another, for the **Sankey** Cup presented by Graham Sankey, players may use only 5 clubs including a putter.

The Club also plays several **matches** each year. The all day matches over 36 holes are against the Oxford & Cambridge GS, Cambridge University Stymies, Oxford University Divots, The Incogniti, the Parliamentary GS, the Forty Club, the Seniors Golfers Society, the Old Marlburians GS and these local Clubs - Betchworth Park, Crowborough Beacon, Royal Ashdown, Wildernesse, and more recently the Dyke. Two Younger members' matches v. Wildernesse and Langley Park are also held. These are all foursomes matches.

The halfday, one round matches include Reigate Heath GC, the Southwark Clergy GS, Limpsfield Chart GC (home and away), Surrey Police, Eastern Division Police, Limpsfield Cricket Club and Gresham Club "A" and "B" teams (both home and away). The President raises a team each year for 18 holes v. Piltdown GC.

Four mixed matches are held over 18 holes against Walton Heath, Piltdown, Widernesse and West Sussex. Internal matches include Ladies v. Men, Ladies v. the Retired Men (twice) and the Committee v. the Staff.

The international rugger match for the Calcutta Cup has become a day when in the morning an England versus Scotland 18 holes foursomes match takes place. After lunch together, the two teams settle down to watch the rugger on the Club's TV. The golf match is for a smart whisky decanter presented by Ian Hume, which the losers are required to fill.

For some years the Chartered Surveyors (led by Barry Cockerell) have challenged the Accountants (led by Ian Blake Thomas) to an annual 18 hole foursomes match, followed by lunch. Since 1997/98, however this match has expanded into a series of **round robin matches** in which teams representing the Chartered Surveyors, the Accountants, the Financiers, the Services, the Medlaws (medics and lawyers) and the Engineers play each other over a series running from November to March. These new internal matches are proving to be a great success, consisting of ten a side foursomes and lunch afterwards. The winners receive the **Peter Skeen** trophy, which is an ancient niblick produced by Alf Baker, given by Peter Skeen.

The large wooden spoon which hangs precariously on the wall near the bar was presented by David Monk and Ian Blake Thomas. It is contested for annually in the **Old v. Young** match in which four teams of ten representing four different age bands play against each other. The loser in the afternoon final take the wooden spoon, and the winners receive the silver spoon donated by Roy Siemssen.

This Old v. Young match started in the 1950's when a team all aged under 30 challeged the over 30s to a match. In an early fixture, a game of spoof started by Philip Jonas after the afternoon round continued for rather a long time, with the loser each time having to down a double whisky. One of the younger players was taken ill on the way home and was arrested for being drunk whilst driving - for which he was subsequently fined and cautioned.

The **Surrey Fives** is a knock-out tournament for Surrey Clubs, each team consisting of five members. Tandridge won this in 1998, with a team comprising Richard Bateman (captain), David Simpson, John Dunbar, Jeremy Garrard and Neil Houlden, with Giles Maberley as an occasional substitute.

The Zig Zag

These Friday morning fortnightly competitions were started in 1970 by the Captain of that year - John Whitlock. Whilst mainly for retired mem, any member is entitled to join in. The format is a 16 hole competition (missing out holes 17 and 18), with members turning up and paying a small entrance fee. Partners are drawn randomly at about 8.45 am.

The competition started as foursomes but in recent years has become a St Andrews' greensome. After playing, members gather in the lounge for a drink and prizegiving. On their 70th birthday, Zig Zaggers are expected to donate a bottle of whisky, but on their 80th birthday they receive a bottle of champagne. There are also awards at the end of the season for the Zig Zagger with the best scores over the year.

Graham Sankey took over the running of the Zig Zag in the mid 1970s and in 1980 the responsibility was passed to Brian Sellman. He was in overall charge for over 15 years until his death, and during that time the competition grew in popularity, with nearly 100 members now taking part. Alec Baker and one of several assistants now run the Zig Zag days.

In 1984 Peter Patchett started the Zig Zag matches which comprise home and away matches against twelve other local Clubs. These matches are now run by Bernard Briault, after Peter's retirement.

The Juniors

Junors at Tandidge began to be encouraged actively during Duncan Ferguson's captaincy in 1979/80, under the leadership then of Mike Holman and John Doubleday. About the same time Bill Stow presented the Club with a capital sum in order to provide an annual prize for the Juniors. Subsequent leaders have been Ted Pocock, John Giggins, John Berry and currently John Crichton.

Various competitions and matches are arranged during the school holidays. One of the most successful young players who has graduated from being a junior has been Tim Slade, now playing off 2 handicap. Another, Peter Rogers, is now scratch.

Juniors may play in two events with their seniors during the year - in the **Parents and Juniors** competition played in the Easter holidays (where the parent need not be a member) and in the **Two Generation** foursomes held in August. Both are 18 holes foursomes stableford. The Juniors also play against a team run by the President for the President's Putter which now hangs in the lounge. Juniors with handicaps of 18 and below are entitled to play in monthly medals/stablefords and in certain other competitions.

Societies

These are welcomed at Tandridge - but only on three days per week i.e. mainly on Wednesdays and Thursdays and to a lesser extent on Mondays. Tuesdays is reserved primarily for the Ladies, and Friday is kept free for Zig Zag events once a fortnight and other matches. Societies currently pay £72.50 for a day's golf at Tandridge. This fee includes an all day green fee, starting times, morning coffee, lunch, and tea or sandwiches.

The office now publishes a monthly bulletin on when tees are reserved for both Societies and Club fixtures, which normally allow friendly Club singles and foursomes to start early each morning. So although the course is very busy - especially from April through to October - members can still play and enjoy their golf.

Social

Although golf continues to be the main, top priority, the social side of the Club has developed considerably in the past few years.

Bridge in particular during the winter months has become popular with a number of members. It began in the 1960's with a duplicate bridge tournament which is still held every year - under Colin Thomas's leadership - at the end of January. It is open to members and guests. In one of the early years, the wife of Graham Mathieson - himself an international bridge player - had her chauffeur sitting by her, said to be learning how to play. A few weeks later the same chauffeur took Graham Mathieson's new, red Rolls Royce off for - he said - a two day service. Neither he nor the Rolls were ever seen again.

It is interesting to see that the notice inviting members to join in the annual dance in the late 1940s, contains the words "A few tables are available for bridge".

Retired men now meet nearly every Friday afternoon during the winter months, for lunch and duplicate bridge under the direction and guidance of Leslie Bailey. A Tandridge team of four - Leslie Bailey, John McKirdy, Colin Thomas and Richard Lovelace - in 1999 got through to the nationwide final of a competition for the best team from any Golf Club. With Catherine Bailey standing in for John McKirdy, they came second, just losing to Porters Park GC.

The Ladies meet similarly every Thursday afternoon for their own games of duplicate, originally under Catherine Bailey but now under Pauline Dunn. The Men and Ladies meet annually in an hard fought duplicate match, usually 24 a side, and played during January.

The Ladies also play duplicate matches against other Clubs in a Downs league - a league which they won for the first time in 1998/99. In February they run a rubber bridge afternoon in aid of a charity chosen by the Lady Captain. This year (1999) nearly 100 members and guests took part and £425 was raised for St Saviour's Priory.

The Club's **Men's Dinner** is nearly always heavily oversubscribed. Suggested by David Ness in 1970, the first Dinner was not held until 1971, when Lord McFadjean was the principal speaker. Subsequent guest speakers years have included the Rt Hon Lord Whitelaw, Rt Hon Lord Bernard Weatherill, Sir Colin Cowdrey, Donald Mosey, Donald Steel, Lord Howie, and many other well known people. A member from the "congregation" has to thank the guest speaker, and some of these speeches have also been memorable e.g. those by Ian Eiloart and by Geoffrey Dove.

By tradition, the guest speaker plays with his host (the Captain) in the Dinner Foursomes the following morning.

A Post-dinner foursome - from l. to r. John Wilson, Mike Holman (the Captain), The Rt Hon Lord Whitelaw and Bob Howie

Dances use to be held twice yearly, one in the Summer and the other over New Year's Eve. In recent years the dances have been held at irregular intervals, depending to some extent on the enthusiasm of the Captain at the time.

TANDRIDGE GOLF CLUB DANCE.

Tickets are limited to 300, so early application is advisable. Each Member may purchase up to 4 tickets.

A few tables are available for Bridge.

There will be a running Buffet including a Cup and soft drinks by Letherby & Christopher Ltd.

There will also be two Bars where other drinks can be obtained at the usual prices.

Dancing to Norman's Band.

Tickets can be obtained from the Secretary, Tandridge Golf Club, Oxted.
Cheques should be made payable to Tandridge Golf Club, crossed Dance a/c.

An invitation to a Dance issued in 1949. Note the facility for playing bridge.

A very successful **Quiz Night** has been held for the past four years, the questions being set by a team from the House Committee past and present. Up to ten teams of eight compete for the prizes and considerable debate usually takes place on the subject on which to play the team's joker (which doubles the points scored). The excellent quizmaster so far has been Tony Skivington.

Burns Night has become another popular celebration since it was started only three years ago by a team from Scotland - including Robert Howie, Ian McIntyre, David Young and Ian Hume. It has all the usual features of a Burns evening such as the presence of a piper, toasting the Haggis, several amusing speeches and a sing-song.

A Race Evening has been held once so far and was much enjoyed by those who attended it. In 1998, **Alex Sizer**, a junior member, gave a fascinating talk about her experience of being a member of the crew of the winning boat in the Round The World yacht race.

No less than six **Christmas lunches** are now provided by William Virley and his team, with two for the Club as a whole, the Ladies, the Zig Zag, the Juniors and a Family lunch for members with young children. All these events are very well supported.

The Men's **Committee Dinner** is held in late November, to mark the end of the Captain's year. The Ladies hold a similar event for their Committee earlier in the year. A few private parties for members and their friends are also held from time to time.

There is to be a **75th Birthday Dinner** on Saturday 5th June this year when 400 members and guests are due to attend.

Other Matters

Gifts by members include the original timber from the deck of Nelson's flagship "HMS Victory" presented by Admiral Sir William Goodenough GCB, MVO, and the Brads clock, fixed to the beam in the lounge, presented in memory of Horace W Elliott - 29 March 1982.

More recently a cricket ball mounted on a plaque was presented by the Incogniti Club to mark the 25th anniversary of their matches against Tandridge. A barometer in the Hall was given by the Coates family in memory of Gordon Coates.

The fascinating glass case by the entrance door to the lounge containing antique clubs and gutta-percha balls was given by the Rev Canon Ken Hoare. The case also holds a left-handed putter presented by Jean Hamilton.

Martin and Guy Sankey, in memory of their father Graham Sankey, presented the large glass cabinet now located in the Gallery Bar. It contains a number of artefacts of the Club, including the golf ball with which Graham holed out two successive 4 irons when playing with Edgar Wren.

The Future

Tandridge today is flourishing. The multitude of caddies in the '30s are no more and have been replaced by trolleys - whether electric or manual - on which to carry the much larger bags. Hickory shafts have given way to steel, then to graphite, boron or other expensive materials. The ball now costs up to £2.50 each but goes further for the average golfer, although the prodigious hits of some of our elders would still take some equalling. Matched sets of irons and increasingly a 5- and 7- wood have replaced the hand made irons and the spoon and baffy. Big Bertha drivers or an equivalent now dominate the golf bag.

The course is longer, the trees much taller and thicker, but there are fewer bunkers to catch our wayward shots. We play less foursomes than we did but still enough to try to ensure that this most enjoyable tradition does not die. Far more of us take a shower after playing than we used to. The camaradarie at the 19th continues unabated.

This book must not close without special reference again to the work of Leslie R Sankey, father of Graham, grandfather of Martin, and great grandfather of Richard and Tim. He was Honorary Treasurer from 1929 until his death in 1936, but was in charge of the finances from before he was elected to the Committee in November 1925. The finances were then in a precarious state. He called an Extraodinary General Meeting and, like a schoolmaster, went through all the figures on a blackboard and answered questions. Then he said "Now gentlemen, you have not come here to decide whether the subscription shall be 6, 8, or any other number of guineas; what you have to decide is whether you want a golf course. If you do, then the subscription will be 10 guineas as I have proved to you."

L R Sankey

Needless to say it was passsed, but even then he had to go round to various members and borrow money to keep Sir Bernard Greenwell at bay. It was thanks to these loans and gifts from a considerable number of members that the mortgage continued to be serviced, and of course to Mr Sankey's strict control and careful nursing of funds. He was convinced that, in the event of failure, the Club might have been run as a business by Sir Bernard and his son, neither of whom were golfers.

Happily his regime of austerity was successful, and the final payment on the mortgage was made on 25th September 1932, and ever since (and hopefully forever) the land has belonged to the members. At the Annual General Meeting in 1932 it was approved that all the gifts and loans received in the time of need would be treated as loans and they were all repaid in a fairly short period. Only then was any capital expenditure allowed.

Let those of us who enjoy our Club and course so much today reflect on what might have happened if it had been turned into a business. Would not some 'developer' have loved to get his hands on the Club's 146 acres for a vast housing estate? Graham Sankey was convinced that we all owe our Tandridge as it is today to his father's work.

BEST SCORE CARDS

Date			Player	H'cap	Gross	Net
9	May	1931	F I S Gill	scr.	70	70
		1938	Jean Hamilton	scr.	68	68
13	Oct	1939	A Waters (pro)	scr.	64	64
11	Oct	1947	W N D Drury	2	70	68
27	Dec	1947	K T Gordon	scr.	70	70
29	Apr	1950	R Siemssen	2	69	67
18	June	1950	Alec Baker (pro)	scr.	64	64
10	Sept	1951	W C Hotton (pro)	scr.	64	64
3	July	1954	G N S Tweeddale	3	70	67
11	Oct	1958	J N E Butcher	4	69	65
28	Mar	1959	F G E Binns	2	69	67
22	May	1960	I MacDonald (pro)	scr.	64	64
18	June	1960	R B Aisher	3	70	67
6	July	1962	N Simmons	3	67	64
29	Sept	1966	Jean Hamilton	6	72	66
2	July	1967	Andrew Phillips	scr.	70	70
2	July	1967	Peter Oosterhuis	scr.	69	69
2	July	1967	Dai Rees (pro)	scr.	70	70
	July	1982	Leslie Hooker (pro)	scr.	69	65
20	April	1985	Jeremy Robson	3	68*	65
8	Aug	1995	Catherine Bailey	3	67*	64

* Course records

Appendix 1

Presidents of Tandridge Golf Club

1925-1940	Sir Bernard Greenwell
1941-1959	Captain C E Hoskins Master
1960-1974	Baron Heyworth of Oxton
1974-1975	Dr E P Andrea
1976-1981	Kenneth Stuart Robinson
1982-1986	Graham Richard Sankey
1987-1993	Robert Spencer Burles
1993-1997	Dr Kenneth Smedley MacLean
1997-	Leslie Thomas Bailey

Captains of Tandridge Golf Club

1925	Benjamin Arthur Cohen KC
1926	Henry D G Leveson-Gower
1927	Stuart Douglas Greig
1928	Sir Ernest M Clarke
1929	Rev Canon John C Morris
1930	Charles I de Rougemont
1931	Admiral Sir W E Goodenough GCB MVO
1932	Sidney Marr Ward
1933	George Herbert Valentine
1934	Leslie Richard Sankey
1935	Walter Lines
1936	Martin S Slattery
1937	Henry Vaughan Letts
1938	Edgar Ronald Grammond
1939	Henry George Marshall
1940	Sir Alfred Parker Sherlock
1941	Geoffrey Heyworth
1942	Harold Gwynne Davies
1943	George Herbert Lawton
1944	Merton Addlestone Jones
1945	Sir Edward Henry Pelham KCB
1946	Arthur Beney OBE
1947	Ralph Estill Huffam MC
1948	Donald Owen Light
1949	Kenneth Stuart Robinson
1950	Alfred Charles Woodhouse
1951	Edward Glanvill Benn
1952	Nathaniel Arthur Jim Cohen

CAPTAINS OF TANDRIDGE taken in 1969

Back row : CJ Whitehead, JB Tanner, WND Drury, PJ Fuller, PG Jonas, KM Evans (Secy.), TA Easton, DF Knight
Middle row : GL Coates, R Siemssen, GR Sankey, IF Stewart, NAJ Cohen, GNS Tweeddale, GT Hankey
Front row : EG Benn, DO Light, Baron G Heyworth of Oxon, W Lines, RE Huffam, KS Robinson.

1953	Walter Neville Dru Drury
1954	Kenneth Gordon McNeil
1955	George Trevor Hankey OBE, TD
1956	Roy Siemssen
1957	Leslie Cartwright Knight
1958	Cecil John Whitehead
1959	John Lawson McConnell MC
1960	Philip Griffith Jonas MC
1961	John Basil Tanner
1962	Graham Richard Sankey
1963	Ian Falconer Stewart
1964	David Francis Knight
1965	Gordon Lionel Coates
1966	George N S Tweeddale
1967	Thomas Aitken Easton
1968	Michael James Monk
1969	Patrick James Fuller
1970	Francis G B Whitlock
1971	Cyril Gordon Stow
1972	Frank Welton Harper
1973	Cecil G W Harrison
1974	Kenneth Stuart Robinson
1975	John D Forbes Watson MBE
1976	Richard Goodwin Rawlings
1977	Robert Spencer Burles
1978	John Hugh Hamer
1979	W Graham Stuart Johnston
1980	James Duncan Ferguson
1981	Robert B A Howie
1982	Anthony T R Nicholson
1983	John Vertue Wilson
1984	Derek Wills
1985	John G Cartwright Knight
1986	John Fletcher Doubleday
1987	Dr Kenneth Smedley MacLean
1988	Philip John Hughes
1989	Guy Andrew M Lyle
1990	Michael Lawrence Holman
1991	John Cox
1992	Ian Robert Eiloart
1993	Air Cdre Philip E Warcup CBE
1994	Gordon Stewart Bisset
1995	Edward George Pocock
1996	Barry John Cockerell
1997	Anthony John Skivington
1998	Peter Jeffrey John Skeen
1999	John Berry

CAPTAINS OF TANDRIDGE in 1999

Back row : SE Kennard (Secy.) IR Eiloart, AJ Skivington, J Berry, PJJ Skeen
2nd row : GS Bisset, B J Cockerell, EG Pocock, ML Holman
Third row : GAM Lyle, J Cox, JF Doubleday, KS MacLean, JGC Knight
Front row : JV Wilson, JD Ferguson, JD Forbes Watson, FW Harper, RBA Howie, PJ Hughes   (Missing: EG Benn, RG Rawlings)

Lady Captains of Tandridge Golf Club

1925	Mrs G F Forwood
1926	Mrs Laming Evans
1927	Miss B Scovell Adams
1928	Mrs L W Alderson
1929	Mrs Laming Evans
1930	Miss E E Whitlock
1931	Mrs A P Meyer
1932	Miss Jean Hamilton
1933	Miss E S Cunningham
1934	Mrs G Leach
1935	Mrs W D Lancaster
1936	Miss E S Cunningham
1937	Mrs L W Alderson
1938	Mrs A C Woddhouse
1939	Miss P Tanner
1940	Miss Jean Hamilton
1941-1946	No appointment
1947	Mrs A C Woodhouse
1948	Mrs L W Alderson
1949	Mrs J L Verrinder
1950	Mrs N A J Cohen
1951	Mrs R M Simon
1952	Mrs L C Knight
1953	Mrs C J Whitehead
1954	Mrs E G Benn
1955	Mrs S V Hicks
1956	Mrs G H Dunbar
1957	Mrs J B Walmsley
1958	Mrs M A Robinson
1959	Mrs R M Simon
1960	Mrs R B Brock
1961	Mrs F G B Whitlock
1962	Mrs T A Easton
1963	Mrs L F Brown
1964	Miss Jean Hamilton
1965	Mrs H W Claxton
1966	Mrs J Oliffe Lee
1967	Miss C J Webster
1968	Mrs A M Monk
1969	Mrs M de Pinna
1970	Mrs G Douglas
1971	Mrs E Rosemont
1972	Mrs E Forbes-Watson
1973	Mrs G Harper
1974	Miss Jean Hamilton

1975	Mrs R Harrison
1976	Mrs P Burles
1977	Mrs D W Ness
1978	Mrs B L Sellman
1979	Mrs R B Howie
1980	Mrs G Bland
1981	Mrs N A J Cohen
1982	Mrs G M Ross
1983	Mrs A T R Nicholson
1984	Mrs E B Bisset
1985	Mrs M L Holman
1986	Mrs H M Turvill
1987	Mrs P A Brown
1988	Mrs C D Thomas
1989	Mrs G R Coy
1990	Mrs D Wills
1991	Mrs P J Hughes
1992	Mrs J G C Knight
1993	Mrs J M Ross
1994	Mrs C M Bailey
1995	Mrs P Parker
1996	Mrs B A Ferguson
1997	Mrs J H T Reynolds
1998	Mrs L Brown
1999	Mrs J C Yule

Appendix 2

Memory of my Early Days At Tandridge

By Alec Baker

To start I have to begin at Limpsfield. My father was assistant at Mitcham Golf Club and in 1910 obtained the position of Professional at Limpsfield Chart.

I was born in April 1915 in the Professional's cottage next to the Club, after my father had left for overseas in World War I. I think I was 3 years old before he saw me. I learned my golf on Limpsfield Chart as a small boy.

When Tandridge was opened in 1924, my father was appointed its first Professional and for a while was Professional of both Clubs as the accommodation at Tandridge was not yet available. He travelled from Limpsfield and back, by bus several days a week, with a large suitcase filled with golf balls, tees, sponges and other small objects, which he set up on the 1st tee to sell.

We moved into the cottage at the entrance when I was 9 years old and my life was taken over by golf - nothing else mattered. Although I did play cricket and football, golf was my sport.

I would sit for hours at the grass knob just over the road at the 1st, listening and watching as my father gave his lessons there. I can well remember too the joy of knocking balls up and down the 1st fairway in the summer evenings.

My father was also a good clubmaker. I had spent hours watching him at Limpsfield and continued to watch and learn at Tandridge. I would sweep up piles of shavings at the end of the day.

At the age of 14 I could not leave school quickly enough, to work in the shop and begin my golfing career. My father was no soft touch as far as work was concerned. My daily chores were to sandpaper the hickory shafts of clubs he was making. They had to be perfectly smooth, were then watered which made the grain rough, then more sandpapering, and more water, until the water did not bring the grain up. They next had to be stained followed by polish, polish and more polish! This procedure also applied to the wooden heads. I had to keep the stock dusted as well as sweep the floors. I soon learned how to put grips on, and also the whipping that went round the necks of the wooden clubs.

I remember becoming the owner of my first steel shaft. A representative of a club firm left behind a sample so I put it on the bench. On his next visit I gave it to him, but he said that although he had missed it, he hadn't been sure where he had left it and that I could keep it. How I treasured that club as it joined my hickory shafts!

I did a lot of caddying in my young days earning the large amount of one shilling and ninepence per round (less than 20p in today's money!). I could still tell some present members of Tandridge what their parents swings were like, and how they were graded among the caddie boys.

Looking at the pictures in the lounge today, I remember little things that happened when caddying for the Captains in the early photographs, then gradually upgrading to playing with others until the present day.

There were so many members and regular visitors of importance in the early days that I am surprised that my father did not get or encourage me to use an autograph book. Here are just a few :

Sport - Cricket	Jack Hobbs
	Brian Valentine
	Maurice Allom
	E R T Holmes, who lived in the big
house	at the bottom of Tandridge.
Sport - Motor Racing	Captain Wolf Barnato, who lived at
	Arden Run
	His Secretary Dale Bourne, who was a
	very good golfer.
Sport - Tennis	Bunny Austin
Film People	Anthony Bushell
	Dorothy Dickson and her daughter
	Dorothy Hyson
	Tony Hancock
	Tony Britton
Other Characters	Winston Churchill
	Lady Churchill

Other Characters	Lord Astor
	Rt Hon Patrick Bowes Lyon (Queen Mary's uncle)
	Prince Arthur of Connaught
	Roy Royston (band leader)

There was a day when the Prince of Wales was expected. The red carpet was laid out and all the Club's officials were ready to receive him. But at the last minute there was a 'phone call saying he was unable to come - a big let down!

I was still at school at the time of the fire which destroyed the clubhouse. I wonder if we would still have a thatched roof clubhouse if it had not been burnt down so early? My father was on the 12th green when he first saw the fire. He rushed back to find volunteers moving his stock on to the grass outside. The firemen were trying to put water on to the side of the shop nearest the clubhouse, without much success because the pressure of water was so low. My father was not pleased as the volunteers' efforts were making all the stock secondhand as it was being thrown down. He wanted to take a chance on the shop burning, which it didn't!

In the middle thirties, several RAF types from Biggin Hill and Kenley used to play. I remember them as a great lot, always happy and cheerful. Among them was Douglas Bader, who after his terrible accident turned up one day, wanting me to play a few holes with him. I thought at first he was joking, but he wasn't, so off we went for what was probably his first game of golf with his tin legs. With the aid of two sticks, which I held while he played his shots, we got along well.

When going up the slope on to the 6th green, he kicked the ground and then had to sit down to refix one of his legs - no problem! When we got to the 14th, we had a discussion as to how to negotiate getting down the bank. I carried a bag on each shoulder, a stick in each bag, and he got behind me, placed a hand on each of my shoulders and we went down very, very slowly without any incident. When I think of it now, it really was quite an achievement.

There were 16 greenkeepers in the early days, Two men did nothing but rake bunkers, one for each 9 holes, 365 bunkers in all. I think the greens were split into 5 or 6 people, each responsible for their allotted greens with - I believe - great competition between them. Mr McDonald was the Head Greenkeeper, and there was a man always in the workshop, tractor drivers and the rest general maintenance men. I can still remember the names of eight of them, but the rest are just faces.

I can also remember the names of several of the regular caddies. There were 40 or 50 on a 9am - 5pm rota run by a caddymaster, a retired army sergeant named Sergeant Millen. There were all types of men : Tink Neves had a clubbed foot; Henry Ellis was a gentleman who had fallen on hard times; Charlie Waterford also came into that category; and Tim Webb who slept in the caddy shed. One whose name I can't remember slept in the shelter that used to be on the right of the second green. Then there was Freddy Glosby who I think ended up as being Tandridge's only caddy. I could write a book on him alone!

One thing I remember enjoying in later years (it must have been during my Army leave after Dunkirk) was when I was asked if I would cut the fairways. Whether I cut them as well as Bert (Moggy) Morris I don't know, but I do know I had fun, going faster than Moggy and sometimes losing one of the cutters in the bunkers! I don't know who cut the fairways after that as I only had time to do them once. I believe sheep did the job for some of the time.

A lady came into the shop one day asking me if I was free to play. I said yes and off we went to the 1st tee. After having two airshots, she finally connected with the ball, hitting it a few yards. She then continued in the same vein all the way down the 1st hole but as we had had to allow several players to come through, the hole took us 90 minute to play! I then suggested that we should play up the 9th, and the same thing happened again - with us letting the same people through as we had done on the 1st hole, and again taking another hour and a half. We agreed to end our game then and when I got back in, my father congratulated me on getting round in three hours. He was a little surprised to hear that we had actually only played two holes.

In 1949 I was appointed Professional to succeed my father.

During my time as Professional, I have happy memories of many friendly matches on a Sunday morning, playing with Bill Hotton (when he was my assistant) against Charles Miles and xxxxx Cook. Later on, in 1966, George Tweeddale started the regular Sunday morning matches between the Captain and me versus challenges from pairs of members.

I gave lessons to many non-members and one or two I remember well. A lady had to travel down from Caterham and despite doing this journey many times, she went up the slip road on to the M25 at Godstone shortly before the motorway was opened. She travelled a long way down the M25 before realising her mistake. When she got to Riverhead, some workmen came to her aid and pushed her car back up the embankment on to the A25, where she resumed her journey back to Tandridge. Her lesson time was up and I could not fit her in, so her morning was wasted. She was not pleased!

There was a girl at the Midland Bank training college (as it was then) by the 15th green. She was a beginner and after her course of lessons, I noticed that there were no players on the 15th and 16th. So I suggested a shot or two on the course to give her a little idea of the difference between the practice ground and the course. We walked over to the 15th tee where I explained what all the different tee boxes were for and teed up a ball for her on the ladies tee. After one or two practice swings, she hit her first shot straight into the hole.......her very first shot, and she did not realise how incredible it was!

Another remarkable thing is that I have seen three holes in one on the same day. I played with a man in the morning when he did a one at the 4th. I partnered him in the afternoon in a fourball when he had another one at the 15th. Then one of our opponents holed out on the 8th - our penultimate hole. I think this must surely be a record. I remember too when Bill Hotton got a two at the 2nd in the morning and hit the pin with his second at the same hole in the afternoon.

My happy times continued until I retired in 1979. Apart from the war years, I would willingly do it all again.